Holly
The Mahogany Girl

Holly
The Mahogany Girl
LESLEY WINTON

First published in Great Britain in 2013 by L & H Publications

First published in paperback in 2013

Copyright © Lesley Winton 2013
Foreword copyright © Ian Hemsley 2013

ISBN-13: 978-1492234340

ISBN-10: 1492234346

Copy Editor - Lisbeth Rieshoj Amos
Cover Design & Copyright © Fiona Newton 2013
Front Cover Photograph - Copyright © Lesley Winton
Back Cover Photograph - Copyright © Phil Wilkinson
Quote on 192 - Copyright © The Pet Crematorium
Quote on Page 195 – Copyright © Linda Macfarlane and
Helen Exley 2003

For Holly

Contents

Dear Reader,

Whether now is the right time or not to begin Holly's story, I don't know. It is only four days since I had to say goodbye to my beloved and constant companion of almost five years and her absence is crushing. Although it feels like time has currently ground to a halt, I know that eventually the weeks and months will begin to pass again and life will gradually return to some form of normality, bringing with it, the inevitable fading of memories.

I don't want to forget and right now, I can't even contemplate moving on and writing about her, keeps her close. It would be a real loss if her story is never told, if the everyday demands of a busy life take over once more, time again becomes scarce and I never get around to writing the only book, I've ever wanted to write.

So I am going to start to write. Perhaps I will be able to see it through, perhaps it will become too painful, but I owe it to my best friend to try.

I know everybody's pet is special but Holly had an extra something, an understanding and a quiet wisdom. An ability to change lives without even realising she was doing it.

Holly and I came into each other's lives when we needed each other the most. We were both broken and we put each other back together again and until the heart-breaking events of May 29th, 2013, we never had a day or night apart in 4 years and 332 days. Abused and neglected during the early years of her life she came to me in a very bad way and in desperate need of help. Our friendship started out with me trying to save her but in actual fact, it ended up being the other way around.

Holly brought more to my life than I could ever give back to her. There is no doubt in my mind that our paths crossed for a reason. The significance of each of us to the other was unquestionable. She was truly my best friend and the best thing that ever happened to me.

This is our story.

Lesley Winton
June 2013

Foreword

The human-canine bond can be a remarkable union and when established, it is forged from love, dependence and trust, on the behalf of both parties. It is a partnership through thick and thin, good times and bad times.

As a small animal veterinary surgeon, I feel privileged to witness and help such partnerships develop over the years. This, I do as part of my professional obligation to uphold the health, wellbeing and welfare of the pets under my care. Occasionally bonds and friendships are formed with both the client and patient that elevate the professional relationship to a special level.

Holly was one such patient who charmed all that knew her and she had a special place in our hearts. We shared the highs and lows of a myriad of clinical conditions that Holly developed over the last few years of her life. Despite the occasional setbacks, Holly always showed resilience and exhibited a wagging tail.

She was a happy dog who gave as much as she received.

This is her story, her life, her legacy.

Ian G. Hemsley BVM&S BSc(hons) MRCVS.

CHAPTER ONE
Before the Sunrise

Having worked in the field of animal welfare for ten years and been an animal lover for as long as I can remember, I have always been aware of the close bond humans can have with their companion animals. Working in this field I was always conscious of how some people could exhibit cruel traits towards animals, but I also never failed to be amazed at the loyalty and devotion that was so often shown by animals towards their humans.

We have dogs that are eyes for the blind and ears for the deaf, assistance dogs that aid the disabled, dogs that can help detect cancer, dogs that serve in the forces and dogs that provide comfort and therapy for the sick, lonely and isolated.

I'll never forget the stories of the two guide dogs that were working in the Twin Towers of the World Trade Centre on the day of the September 11th, 2001 terrorist attacks. One of them led his master down seventy flights of stairs to safety and the second was released by his trapped owner so the dog could have some chance of saving himself. The dog refused to leave. How often is such devotion shared between people?

Dog ownership wasn't new to me. I got my first dog, Tulsa, when I was eighteen after my mother endured much pestering from me and finally relented after my sister left home to get married. Prior to that and at every opportunity possible, I would walk and look after neighbours' and friends' dogs. Tulsa was with us for ten years and after his death in 1992, this pattern continued due to the fact that my work circumstances didn't enable me to have a dog of my own. Much as I wanted my own dog, I wasn't going to get one if it meant leaving it on its own for hours on end while I worked.

For around ten years up to 2004, I worked for the wonderful charity the World Society for the Protection of Animals (WSPA), initially as a volunteer and then as their Regional Co-ordinator for Scotland. Although based at home, I travelled around Scotland raising funds and awareness for their animal protection work around the world. I adored this job. In fact, it didn't feel like a job, more like a passion. I put my heart and soul into it until a change in management and a centralisation of UK work in London resulted in my being made redundant and the Scottish Office being closed.

Devastated, didn't even begin to describe how I felt.

Since leaving school, I'd always been pretty certain which career path I wanted to take. I loved Law – I always imagined myself as a bit of a hot shot lawyer, standing up in court arguing for justice and fighting for the underdog, no doubt a glamorized view of courtroom life from watching too many episodes of *L A Law* and *Law and Order* in the 80's. I went to college and enrolled in Legal Studies and Business Studies courses and after qualifying, I spent the next fifteen years working for legal firms. The reality was never as exciting as the dream.

Throughout these years, in my spare time, I became more and more involved in animal welfare and when the opportunity of part time employment with WSPA arose coinciding with my dwindling interest in the world of law, my decision to embark on a complete career change was an easy one. Despite the fact that it meant taking a substantial salary cut, the value of following my heart outweighed the value of money. It was a natural progression, chasing the next dream.

So when I was made redundant some ten years later, having always been confident and certain about what I wanted to do in life at each stage, for the first time since leaving school, I was left adrift. I couldn't imagine working in any other area than animal welfare and I knew with complete certainty that I didn't want to go back into the legal field. I lived on my own, with a mortgage and bills to pay and for the first time in twenty years of being part of the UK workforce, I suddenly had no job, no income and no security. The redundancy payment I received was the legal minimum which if I was lucky, would last a few weeks. I only had a very small pot of savings to fall back on and credit cards if required. I had one life policy which, since I had no children, I decided to cash in as I thought the money would be of more use to me at that juncture. It would buy me a little time while I worked out what I wanted to do next and got back on my feet again.

Redundancy is a horrible experience. Apart from the obvious financial implications, it's very hard not to take it personally and start wondering what you did wrong and if you weren't good enough. Because my job was based at home, I had converted my spare room into an office and I had been given four weeks to wind the whole operation up. Sadly this meant, it wasn't as simple as clearing out my desk, putting my belongings in a box and walking out of the office. I had to dismantle my home office in time for the removal men who would arrive in a few days to take everything back to London. The fact that all this had to be done a couple of days before Christmas made the impact all the harder.

The sadness engulfed me. I felt I'd lost my identity and my direction. Everything I felt was stable and secure had disappeared. This led to a downward spiral of depression and ill health that I felt would never end. I became angry and distraught at the circumstances I found myself in and this was compounded by the heartwrenching breakdown of one of my longest and closest relationships, around the same time, which made the weight of my despair almost unbearable. I fell into the trap of using alcohol, as so many people do, to try and numb painful emotions, but all that achieved was to plunge me deeper and deeper into depression and make a bad situation worse. I began to self-destruct.

I got myself in a terrible mess, which in hopeless despondency culminated in my taking an overdose. It was a very black and bleak time in my life, one that is painful even now to recall. I didn't want to die, I just felt worthless, useless, desperately unhappy and a total failure. My life had disintegrated and I just wanted the pain to stop, if only for a little while.

Often when we fall on difficult times or life deals us one of its crushing blows we hear the old faithful platitudes 'don't worry, everything happens for a reason' and 'every cloud has a silver lining,' along with 'you'll look back and this will be the best thing that ever happened to you.' People mean well and they are trying to help but when you hit rock bottom, it's hard to see any light at the end of the tunnel or any glimmer of hope.

After travelling to London for my farewell get-together with my work colleagues after my redundancy, I will never forget the words of the taxi driver who brought me back to my hotel at the end of the evening. I was tired and emotional and poured my heart out to him. He patiently listened to me unburdening my heartache then quite simply said….'Don't worry, the sun will rise again tomorrow.'

And it did…and it shone brighter than I could ever have imagined.

HOLLY, THE MAHOGANY GIRL

CHAPTER TWO
Driving Forward

My first priority to dig myself out of my black hole was to find another job - if not a new career, at least another source of income. My bills weren't going to pay themselves and I couldn't exactly pay my mortgage with magic beans. I had to think and think fast. Although very unsure of which way I wanted to go, I was certain of two things. I no longer wanted to work for an employer and driving was one of my greatest pleasures.

At the time, there were many adverts around for training to be a driving instructor. They promised a good and stable income (don't believe everything you hear!) and I thought I had my answer – a way forward and a focus for the future. So I began my training. After many, many weeks and months of study, training and practice and a lot of fees later, I passed all three exams to become a fully qualified driving instructor in 2006. I had taken a number of part time jobs from private chauffeuring to office administration to tide me over until I qualified.

The way the system worked at that time, you could go on a 'trainee' badge to gain experience with real learners before qualifying. Although I found this an extremely helpful process and one I felt should be compulsory, the fact that you could, in effect, charge more than a qualified instructor if you wanted to and had no legal obligation to tell your pupil you weren't fully qualified, was one of many anomalies and peculiarities about the profession that began to trouble me at an early stage. Having myself struggled to get through the third and final of the three exams required to qualify, when I heard there was only a pass rate of around 18% - 20% nationwide for part three, it was even more demoralizing.

I couldn't understand how pass rates could possibly be so low. Also during my training, I discovered that the people who examined potential instructors of the future didn't have to have been instructors themselves and, indeed, they could be people who had tried to train to become an instructor themselves but failed, was another reason I became a bit disheartened. I felt that would be like a learner driver telling another learner if they were good enough to pass. After two years of studying and thousands of pounds of tuition fees later, which I could ill afford at the time, I found it very hard to reconcile the fact that the person who would decide if I was good enough to be a driving instructor or not, could well be someone who didn't make the grade themselves. Just two of the elements of the job that I struggled with then and still do now.

However, after a long slog, I passed all the exams and for the first time since my redundancy, I felt that I had a clear way forward. I began to establish my business and build up my pupil base. It was a start.

Due to the nature of my business, my clientele was predominantly around seventeen and eighteen years of age and I learned very quickly that this wasn't the most reliable client base! If they'd had a heavy night in the pub the night before their lesson, they'd cancel. Many a time I would be waiting outside their house to pick them up, only to find they had slept in or mysteriously forgotten they had a lesson. So unfortunately the job didn't bring the financial security I craved.

While teaching, I learned very quickly to fine tune my communication skills. 'Slow down quicker' produced interesting results and 'brake gently,' was quickly replaced with 'gently brake' after one too many abrupt stops. 'Go straight over at the roundabout', was rapidly, rephrased to 'keep to the left lane throughout and take the second exit' just in case the pupil took me too literally and drove straight over the roundabout, which unfortunately, wasn't beyond the realms of possibility.

The job also gave me a real insight into different elements of society. At one point I had a seventeen year old pupil who already had two children and was pregnant with her third. I worried greatly about some of my young female pupils who were in abusive relationships and very quickly I felt like a counsellor and social worker as well as their instructor. At the other end of the scale I would have pupils in their seventies who needed refresher courses after being widowed and were desperately trying to regain some independence for the remainder of their lives. There were some really funny times too and times when my careful use of words would go horribly wrong. On one occasion while teaching one of my loveliest boys who was extremely effeminate and a great joy to teach, I just don't know what I was thinking when I told him to put his handbag on instead of his handbrake. I'm so pleased he saw the funny side. I'll also never forget an introductory telephone call I made to a new pupil. His mother answered and I asked to speak to him, the reply was 'Hang on, he's outside with his birds'. Good grief, I thought, how many women does a seventeen year old boy have? Turned out, he bred budgies.

Anyway with the good and the bad, the job provided me with an income albeit not a stable one, but it helped me deal with my most immediate problem of having to earn a living. It gave me foundations to build on for the next few years.

Despite losing my much loved job in animal welfare in 2004, I never lost my love of animals and my desire to help them. Although I loved all animals and abhorred any form of cruelty, I always had a great love for bears and dogs. I continued to fundraise for organisations such as Animals Asia and their vital work to end bear farming and the Idaho Black Bear Rehabilitation Center and their incredible work to rescue cubs orphaned, often as a result of their mothers being shot by hunters. The Center would take these orphans in and nurture and care for them until they were big enough and strong enough to be returned to the wild, for a second chance at life.

In 2008, I was given the incredible opportunity to travel to Idaho to help return twenty-one black bear cubs to the wild. I knew come hell or high water, I had to go and it was to prove one of the best things to ever happen in my life.

The best thing, would happen shortly afterwards.

HOLLY, THE MAHOGANY GIRL

CHAPTER THREE
First Impressions

During those early years as a driving instructor, I learned that I would often form close relationships with my pupils. Depending on their ability, some would be with me for a relatively short time and others would be with me for quite a few months. I would get to know them well and they would get to know me. Indeed, some have remained firm friends, long after passing their tests.

Despite the job's ups and downs, it had brought with it a working pattern that would at last allow me to get another dog. I don't know why, but I had always wanted a black Labrador. I think I was drawn to that breed as my first dog had been a cross between a Labrador and a Collie and many of the dogs I'd looked after had been Labs or Lab crosses. They were such lovely natured dogs and best of all, they were a large breed. I always adored big dogs – you could get a great cuddle from them!

I became aware of a golden Labrador through in the West of Scotland that was looking to be re-homed.

There were five children in the family and no room for the dog. It really breaks my heart when dogs or any animals for that matter are so often treated as disposable assets. I know as well as anyone what hard work they can be and the financial implications but to take them on, love them, care for them, make them part of your family just to get rid of them when they are too much trouble or an inconvenience, is something I have never been able to comprehend. However, at least this family were trying to do the right thing and they weren't just throwing the dog out onto the streets. They were trying to find him a loving home.

I went to visit him and he was really gorgeous, extremely boisterous but a beautiful loving dog. There was no doubt he was a handful but he would have been a wonderful family pet. But he wasn't black – I really wanted a black Labrador. What was wrong with me? Was I a doggie racist?!

My mind is a little blurred here as I try to recollect the order of things. I think, by this point, I had already met Holly, very briefly. One of my pupils had been helping a friend of one of her family members with the care of a black Labrador they had recently taken on, but were struggling with. The dog was being left on its own for long, long periods of time and not getting the care and attention it needed.

After dropping her off after a lesson, my pupil said 'come and meet Holly' - little did I know where this would lead. I think this must have been early 2008. She was a beautiful, beautiful looking dog. She must have been a pedigree; she didn't look like she was crossed with anything. On further inspection, she had quite a lot of bald, dry patches on her skin and when I put my hand forward to pat her, she pulled away, unusual for a Lab – known as a friendly, cheerful breed. I didn't feel her reaction was that of a dog that may have been hit before more I felt that of a dog that hadn't experienced much affection in her life – hadn't experienced it and didn't know how to show it or react to it when offered.

I enquired more about her background and was told she'd been passed from pillar to post and had four or five different homes in as many years. She had been used as a breeding machine, never exercised and kept in a cage that was far too small for her. This, I thought, may explain all the rough patches on her skin, pressure sores of sorts.

Something was mentioned about her coming from Labrador Rescue but she wasn't spayed so I felt this couldn't have been the case, as I believed shelters always spayed or neutered their dogs before being re-homed, but to this day, I know no more about Holly's life before she came to me other than the vague details I was given. I couldn't verify anything and had no records for her. I couldn't even be sure of her age as there was no date of birth, but we thought she must be around four or five years old and the first vet I took her to confirmed that.

Brief as it was, that was Holly's and my first meeting, nothing remarkable at the time, but I would come to look back on it with an element of incredulity the next time we met.

CHAPTER FOUR
Walking Barrel

Just before I went to Idaho in 2008, I offered to look after Holly for a weekend to help out. I hadn't seen her since our first meeting and had been thinking long and hard about committing fully to dog ownership again. The thought crossed my mind that I could offer to look after Holly for a few days and this would be a good way to ease myself back in. No-one should underestimate the responsibility of taking on a dog and this should never be done lightly. They can be a tie, they need regular exercise, stimulation and a good diet, their veterinary needs must be met along with the resulting fees and more often than not, you will outlive them, bringing the inevitable grief and sadness at the end of their lives. However, I have always been a firm believer that provided you give all these matters due consideration and accept them, the great joy and love you get in return from giving a dog a home, outweigh any of the difficulties tenfold.

So, I made the telephone call to offer to look after

Holly the following weekend, and her carer at the time snapped up my offer. They told me they'd drop her off on the Friday and happened to add 'just to forewarn you, Holly's got really fat since you last saw her.' No problem, I thought, we'll have some lovely long walks together. It will do us both good.

Friday arrived and I readied the house, moving any fragile items that could be knocked over by an over-enthusiastic dog and their waggy tail and awaited Holly's arrival. Then I looked out of the window and will never forget the sight that greeted me. A great big furry rotund black barrel on legs waddled towards my door. Her head was bowed and her brow drooped. She lumbered across my front grass, looking more like a bear than a dog, struggling to put one paw in front of the other and panting heavily from the exertion of simply moving. She struggled through my front door and was no sooner in when she slumped down in the middle of the living room floor, completely spent from the effort of getting from the car, parked mere feet away, to the house.

I was utterly gobsmacked. I could barely react or find the right words. I knelt beside Holly, giving her a big hug followed by 'Hello girl'. This time she didn't even draw away as she had the first time we met, she had no energy to do even that. I couldn't bring myself to say 'How are you' as it was clear, this dog was struggling and in dire need of help. Her toys, bedding and bowls were left with me and I couldn't help but feel, this dog can hardly walk, never mind play with toys.

What on earth had happened? The slim, svelte dog I had met a few months ago had vanished. Her face and body had distorted so much that she didn't even look like the same dog. She could barely lift her head and there was no sign of any wag in the tail or any zest for life. The folds of skin over her brow made her look all the more miserable as it fell into her eyes, which must have affected her sight. My heart broke for Holly. I was no lightweight myself but that was my fault, Holly didn't feed herself, she relied on her human to decide on her diet. Had they been ordering pizza for her every night?

I really was so shocked. Not just in the change of appearance but in the overall deterioration of the dog. She was so despondent, so subdued, so beaten by the simple task of moving. It just looked like she'd had enough. Whatever this poor dog had to endure in the years up to that point seemed to emanate from her entire being as she lay slumped, motionless, on my living room floor.

Poor Holly. My plans for lovely long walks during our weekend together were out of the question. The best we could manage were short walks, close to home. I learnt very quickly to bear in mind whatever distance we walked, we still had to get home. She tired so easily, I had to ensure she conserved enough energy for the walk back to the house. It was truly heart-breaking. Back home I would try to play with her and generate a little interest in her toys, all to no avail. All she wanted to do was lie in a heap on the floor.

The weekend slipped by in a docile daze and soon it was time to return Holly to her owner. I had my trip to America coming up or I would have kept her longer. It broke my heart to let her go and I couldn't help but fear for her future.

CHAPTER FIVE
Bear with Me

My trip to Idaho to help return orphaned bear cubs to the wild was one of the most memorable experiences of my life. The only difficult part of it was the long journey there. It involved flights from Edinburgh to Amsterdam, Amsterdam to Minneapolis, then a short flight from Minneapolis to Idaho. All in all, I was travelling for around thirty hours. It was so tiring and uneventful, until the last leg of the journey. The travel schedule included a five-hour stopover in Minneapolis airport before a short three-hour flight to Idaho.

During this wait, the weather very kindly decided to whip up a few tornadoes. The impact of these tornadoes would make the news around the world and would prove devastating for the Little Sioux Scout Ranch in a remote part of Iowa. One of the tornadoes touched down in this area minutes after a warning was issued and resulted in a number of fatalities and many injuries. Tornadoes also touched down in southern Minnesota and eastern

Nebraska as residents and officials battled against rising flood waters. The unfolding events were being played out on TV sets all around the airport as the ferocious winds and torrential rain started to batter the airport building windows to a background cacophony of thunder and lightning. Our departure time was fast approaching and there were tornadoes all around us. Scared of flying at the best of times, I was petrified.

An announcement came over the tannoy saying that the pilots of our plane had been delayed arriving from their previous flight, but were 'running through the airport' as the announcement was being made so that they could get our flight away in the closing half an hour window before they had to shut the airport and ground all flights because of the weather.

I was filled with relief and terror in equal measures. I was desperate to reach Idaho as it had been such a long time since I'd left Edinburgh but the weather was horrendous and never in my life had I been on a plane in such dreadful conditions, there was part of me that would far rather have stayed on the ground.

The closest I'd come in the past to flying in a storm was after a trip to Canada when during take-off on the journey home, our plane was struck by lightning during our ascent. The blinding flash and ear shattering bang would have sent me running to the nearest exit if we hadn't been at 10,000 feet. I'd never been in a plane hit by lightning before and apparently, although very common, it was unusual to be hit at a low altitude. I was convinced we'd lost an engine and we were just at the beginning of our very long flight back over the Atlantic. I think I must have held my breath the whole way home expecting something dreadful to happen.

As our pilots sprinted across the terminal, we boarded the plane. A short while later, with rain battering off the fuselage windows, strapped into my seat and gripping on to the arm rests for dear life, we taxied to the runway to prepare for take-off. I can only describe the next few minutes by likening it to taking off in a blender.

To a seasoned traveller it was probably no more than a rough ascent but for me, I was certain this was when I would meet my maker and I would never reach my destination and my much longed for visit to the bear sanctuary. This take-off of terror continued for what seemed like an eternity despite reassurance from the pilot that we were just climbing above the storm clouds to calmer air. Then it stopped. The buffeting and tossing around of the plane in the blender eased and the most calming, peaceful and awesome sight appeared outside my window. We had dark clouds above us and below us and this light, bright sliver of calm in between the two where we were now flying. It was like a cloud sandwich with our plane as the filling. Thankfully the remainder of the flight was calm and uneventful and over thirty hours after leaving Edinburgh, I arrived in Boise, Idaho to the lovely words of the lady than runs the sanctuary as she announced 'Scotland's in Town!'

I would spend the next ten days helping return

twenty-one beautiful young black bears of all shapes and sizes back to the wild. The bears had been orphaned, often as a result of their mothers being shot by hunters or they had been killed in road traffic accidents and the cubs had been taken in by the Idaho Black Bear Rehabilitation Center. There, they were nursed back to health until big and well enough to be returned to the wild. My job would be to help weigh, measure, tag, collar, hoist on stretchers and lift the bears into their transportation crates for their journey home. As the bears weighed anything from 50lbs to 200lbs, this particular task swung from being relatively straightforward to providing a major challenge.

Over the next three days, with the bears safely in their travel crates on the back of the truck, we would travel over six hundred miles of rugged, dirt road terrain, twisting and turning high up and around the sides of hills and mountains with sheer drops to the side to deep lakes below. With my heart in my mouth, I couldn't help but think 'If we're going to go over – please make it on the way back, so at least the bears are safe.'

It was an astounding experience to be part of returning these incredible animals back to the wild for a second chance at life and one that cemented my determination to one day set up my own charity for bears.

On the journey home to Scotland, I reflected on the events of the last few weeks. The fulfilment of one long held dream to do hands-on work with bears and the gradual steps taken to fulfil another dream of getting a dog.

Shortly after I returned home, my mobile phone bleeped with an incoming text message. It was from Holly's current owner, and the message read 'Hope you had a lovely holiday. Things are very hectic here. Please don't feel you have to but I was wondering if you would like to take Holly… permanently'.

HOLLY, THE MAHOGANY GIRL

CHAPTER SIX
New Arrival

I read the text for a second time and digested its content. I thought back to the weekend I'd had with Holly before going to Idaho and felt overwhelmed as I recalled this poor downtrodden, miserable dog. How could I not take her in? If I didn't, I don't think she would live much longer and if she did, it would be days of misery that would simply be endured with little pleasure. I had to think. I had to be level headed and sensible. I couldn't let my heart rule my head. The responsibility of taking on a dog should never be taken lightly and should always be thought through carefully. I would be taking on a very poorly dog that would need more than the usual level of care and attention. I still had big money worries accumulated from my redundancy and now I had my Idaho trip to pay off the plastic too. There were bound to be substantial veterinary fees involved with caring for Holly. Even with insurance cover, there were always excesses and items that wouldn't be covered under the policy.

I'd looked into the possibility of getting help via the PDSA, which is the animal equivalent of the UK National Health Service, but found that it was only for people on benefits and didn't cover people on a low income. That always amazed me as I'd done work experience at the PDSA when I was at school and recalled the number of pet owners who arrived in the car park in their 4 x 4's and flash cars. It didn't seem quite right to me! All I could think about were all these poor dogs in shelters that needed help and couldn't be helped because potential owners with a low income weren't eligible for help from the PDSA but couldn't get insurance for whatever reason. Luckily, I was able to get insurance for Holly and I would find a way somehow financially.

Holly's main problem was her weight. When I'd initially met her only a few months earlier, she was slim and sleek and otherwise healthy. As with so many rescued dogs, I could never be one hundred percent certain of her history and would never be able to fully verify what I had been told about her former life.

Her rapid deterioration had taken place over only a matter of months and I could reverse it. Why write the poor girl off because she was a bit portly? There was very little I could do to help her in the short weekend we'd had together but if she was with me permanently, with the correct veterinary guidance and a good diet and exercise regime, I could really help her. We'd get fit together – we'd be good for each other. One thing I knew for certain was that this dog needed help and she needed it now. My mind was made up.

I picked up my mobile, opened the text message up again and hit the reply button, 'I'd love to', I typed, 'Can she come on June 30th?'

'Yes', came the reply.

Excitedly, I readied myself and the house for the new arrival. I quietly, with a tinge of sadness, laughed at my efforts before Holly's last visit to move ornaments and valuables that may be knocked over by an enthusiastic dog. Knowing now that it would be nothing short of a miracle if she could muster up the strength to wag her tail, never mind knock anything over.

As soon as my decision was made to take Holly, I knew it was the right one, for her and for me. Although things had improved for me considerably over the last few years with qualifying in my new profession and having my lovely America trip, I was still suffering from bouts of depression and wasn't looking after myself as well as I should have been.

Shortly after my redundancy, I had been diagnosed with reactive depression as a result and it was taking a lot longer than I expected to get on top of this. I was still on antidepressants and although I fully understand and appreciate that there is definitely a place for them as and when needed, for me, I couldn't help but feel it was still a sign of my failure. I would never say that to anyone else, but I always tended to be really hard on myself. I had to take the last few steps to pick myself up and move on and the only person who could do that for me was me.

Very soon I would have responsibilities, someone else would be depending on me and looking to me to care for them and look after them, so I had to be strong now. After all, Holly needed me.

I prepared special areas around the house for Holly so she could get her bearings when she arrived in her new home and could settle in at her own pace. I put her food and water bowls in the kitchen and made up a toy box in the living room, where I also laid out her bed area. I could only begin to imagine what would be going on in her head if this was her fifth or sixth home in only four or five years. The very first thing I wanted to offer her was stability and routine. The next, love and lots of it.

June 30th, arrived and Holly's owner dropped her off with a few of her old toys before leaving. 'Hi Holly', I said, 'Welcome to your new home!'

She looked at me with her big brown eyes, puzzled, sad and weary, weighed down by her furrowed brow. Then she flopped down on the floor, front paws stretched out, resting her head on them. It was clear that absolutely everything was far too much effort for her.

We settled into our first day together and shortly before bedtime, attempted a little walk up to the grassy area at the top of our street. Holly lumbered and waddled her way there, head held low, tail drooping, every step an endurance for her. She relieved herself and we started the journey back home. The house was minutes away but to Holly, it must have felt like a marathon. It was heart-breaking to see her struggle so much. It was clear that we had a long journey ahead of us, but we had taken the first steps together, literally.

When we got home and settled down for the evening, much to my surprise, my new housemate managed to heave herself up on to the couch to sit beside me. It was her own decision which took her a bit of time and effort but the determination on her face was clear. She stood looking at me, then looking at the empty, inviting spot on the couch next to me and after shuffling from one front paw to the other while she was clearly working out the easiest route up, one front paw went up, closely followed by the second. She rebalanced and regrouped and then did the same with her back legs – shuffling one, then the other closer to the couch. Then with great accuracy and dexterity for such a large dog she lifted one back leg up onto the front ridge of the couch and with great determination dragged the fourth leg up and with a thump down beside me, her mission was complete. She then manoeuvred her upper body and front paws round so she was facing me and finally landed on top of my lap.

I had always hoped she would be a couch dog – I never had any issues about dogs on furniture but given her condition, I was never going to force her. I was really very moved that after such a short time, she felt comfortable enough to snuggle in. Snuggle perhaps was the wrong word – crush may well have been more appropriate. Bearing in mind, this dog weighed at least seven stone and as she made herself comfortable lying over my legs, digging her elbows in to me, there was an understandable element of discomfort on my part. However, I didn't care, I couldn't have been happier.

As we relaxed and Holly drifted off to sleep, she started snoring. The poor old girl had so many excess folds of skin weighing heavily around her neck and nasal passages, she really had fairly major issues with this socially questionable trait – never endearing in a lady. At times she would build to such a crescendo, the TV volume would have to be turned up to counteract her increasing decibels as her snoring escalated. In fact, it often went a step further to the point where I was convinced she must have the canine version of sleep apnoea.

While she made herself comfortable sprawled out over my lap as my legs went numb, the snoring would continue, getting louder and louder. Her muzzle would vibrate, nostrils flare, jowls flap and flop and the walls felt like they would come tumbling down and then suddenly, it stopped. Silence. Nothing. No body movement. Deathly still. What on earth happened? Had she died? There was nothing else for it but to give her a sharp prod which thankfully would then result in an enormous, rip roaring snort that any pig would be proud of, one which came frighteningly close to inhaling the contents of the living room and she was off again, contentedly resuming her snoring and the TV would be turned up a little bit more.

It was sad and comical in equal measures, but she was relaxed and happy and that was the main thing.

HOLLY, THE MAHOGANY GIRL

CHAPTER SEVEN
Weighty Matters

My first priority was to get Holly to a vet for a thorough check up. I made an appointment with our local surgery as soon as I could get one. The day of our appointment arrived and with a carefully engineered push and a shove, I managed to get Holly into the car and we made our way to the vets. We walked into reception and everyone's jaws dropped. None of them, not the receptionists, the nurses nor the vets had ever seen such a big dog. I think that was the moment the full extent of Holly's predicament hit me.

The first thing they did was put her on the scales. As the numbers rapidly spun through their sequence, going up and up they finally stopped…. 62kg… TEN STONE! My guesstimate of seven stone was way off. I could have cried, in fact, I think I did. How could anyone let a dog get in this state? I know I was probably imagining it, but despite explaining the circumstances that had brought us here, I couldn't help but feel that everyone there must have thought I'd done this to Holly, that she had been my dog all along, that I'd been negligent in her care and decided out of guilt that perhaps she should see a vet. In hindsight, I know that wasn't the case but it was a horrible situation and I felt thoroughly miserable but my focus had to be Holly.

She was taken into the consulting room where they took blood to run some tests to see if there were any other problems we had to contend with and we would get the results back in a few days.

I talked everything through with the vet and we formulated a diet and exercise plan. Because of Holly's size it had to be little and often – both her food and her walks. Small regular meals would kick-start her metabolism and gentle exercise daily with perhaps one or two slightly longer walks through the week would gradually improve her fitness. As my poor downtrodden dog sat slumped in the corner of the consulting room as we discussed her future my heart ached for her. She'd never asked for any of this and had already been through so much in such a young life. My bond with her was really growing even after only a matter of days.

As we left the surgery with an enormous bag of prescription diet dog food, I had to develop a whole new skill – negotiating keeping a door open with my foot, while handling a ten stone dog with one arm and carrying a 12kg bag of dog food with the other, it crossed my mind that my fitness levels would soon be improving too.

We returned home and decided we'd get our exercise

regime off to a good start and drive down to the local beach. It would be a change of scenery for Holly and she may even manage a little paddle. It would be nice for her to experience the sensation of sand and water on her dry paws and it was a beautiful sunny day. We headed off with me at the wheel and Holly navigating from the back seat, watching the passing scenery with interest. We arrived at the beach car park and my passenger clambered out of the car as soon as I opened the door. My heart skipped a beat – had I imagined it or was there a tiny hint of enthusiasm there? I almost dared not hope, but as she began to waddle towards the path to the beach, there was a teeny, tiny hint of a spring in her step. It was a great sign.

Because of her bulk, Holly tired very easily and wherever we went, I always had to remember we had to get back. The tide was out so after padding around in the sand for a while, I decided it was too far to attempt to get her down to the water. I promised her that next time we'd come, we'd be able to reach the water and we started the short walk back to the car. It was a warm day and Holly was beginning to show signs of real fatigue. We reached the car and she sat down heftily on her bottom somewhat lopsided and balancing her body against the car wheel, panting heavily. I poured some water into her bowl, but even drinking that was too much effort. I gave her a cuddle and said, 'Come on girl, let's just go home and you can have a good rest, you've had a busy day.' If I thought the day had been a bit of a struggle already, my next challenge was to prove even more difficult.

I couldn't get Holly to budge. She seemed quite content to sit propped up by the car to recharge her batteries. Nothing I tried worked. I couldn't get her to stand, never mind climb into the car and lifting her was out of the question. We were stuck. By this time it was around 5pm and I had visions of us being stranded in the car park all night and it wasn't the most savoury place to be at night-times.

As I pondered my next move, I decided to ring my mother. I hadn't caught up with her for a while and we weren't going anywhere fast. To my mum's great amusement, I explained to her my current dilemma. We debated possible solutions and even entertained the thought of contacting a local crane company to ask for a helping hand.

We were in quite a pickle. Then mum came up with the brilliant suggestion of opening both back doors of the car and trying to entice Holly in from the other side. If I could encourage her enough from one side of the car to get her front paws in, I could then run round the other side of the car to lift her rear end in. I don't know if it was the brilliance of mum's idea or that Holly had had time to regain her strength while we'd been formulating our plan, but it worked.

I relayed the good news to mum and with a massive sense of relief, Holly and I headed home after what would be one of our many eventful days together.

CHAPTER EIGHT
Morning Cuddles

Over the next few weeks and months Holly made great progress, as did I. We both began to lose weight and our walk distances gradually increased. We had become quite a talking point in the neighbourhood as we became a familiar sight on walks and the neighbours started to witness Holly's transformation. I remember one neighbour recalling seeing us in the early days walking past her window painfully slowly, every step laborious for Holly - then she suddenly caught sight of us a few months later and thought 'Goodness, look at the speed they're going!' Holly was never really built for speed, even after her weight loss at best, when attempting to run she would manage a floppy gallop, but it was a clear sign of our progress.

There were not so nice comments as well. As we walked together, two rather generously proportioned ladies, complete strangers would shout, 'That dog needs to go on a diet and you could do with one too', followed by looks of disgust as they walked away.

It was so hurtful and I was really shocked that people could be so nasty and judgemental with no knowledge of the circumstances. Sadly, it became a regular occurrence and as my frustration and anger grew along with my intense feelings of protectiveness towards Holly, I began to stop these people and engage in conversation. I felt, if you have time to insult my dog, you can take time to listen to her story. From that point on, people began to take note of and comment on her progress and how well she was doing. Perhaps between us, Holly and I taught a few people not to judge by appearances.

Attitudes didn't change overnight and I will never forget one instance in the early days where again, my heart bled for Holly. I was really beginning to feel like a proud parent revelling in every little success and step forward their 'child' made and when the child took a knock, so did the parent. The initial blood tests from the vets had shown that Holly was suffering from hypothyroidism. It was impossible to tell if this may have caused her weight gain or been as a result of it but she was put on the correct medication to manage it – very similar to humans with a thyroid problem. It may well have explained her lethargy too. Thankfully, the blood tests showed nothing more serious. I felt that with her new diet, exercise regime and medication we were on the right track and really making progress. I always tried to keep Holly moving and we had developed a morning routine that included what we called 'morning cuddles' where I rubbed and rubbed her back, bottom and tummy.

She loved it and if I didn't do it quickly enough in the morning she would often push me over so I fell onto the couch to administer this much loved treatment a bit quicker. My reasoning behind it was that I wanted to get her circulation going and get her stimulated and energised at the beginning of the day. Whether this worked or not, I'm not sure, but she loved it. Perhaps the reason for her glee was a bit of relief for a dry skin caused by her thyroid problem or simply the joy of touch and affection at last, which had been sadly lacking in her life up to that point. This routine became a great source of joy for us both and as Holly's health was to improve, it graduated into a ritual that would see her charging through my legs head first to get her bottom rubbed then coming back through the other way to get her tummy rubbed, tail wagging madly as I felt she would burst with joy. This became a game that she insisted playing with every visitor to the house, much to their surprise at times but great amusement. This was all fine until our visitors were wearing skirts! We then ran the very real risk that Holly may end up running round the room with a guest riding on her back. Despite the obvious risk of an embarrassing outcome, it was a game she and I loved playing together and it was one of many steps in the right direction to put this sweet dog back together again.

The incident that always sticks in my mind from the early days when Holly was still extremely large and docile happened at our local supermarket. Holly and I were accompanying our friend to do her weekly shopping. As I always liked to try and keep Holly active, we got out of the car but had to wait at the door.

Holly plonked herself down at my feet shifting her portly frame to find the most comfortable position, folds and layers of body fat settling into place, with a tired and exhausted expression on her face. Alongside her sat the most perfectly groomed and manicured cocker spaniel, striking poses as if auditioning for Crufts, while waiting for her owner. As Holly and I waited for our friend, customers came and went. Without fail, every single one of them gravitated towards the perfectly presented cocker, who was flaunting her good looks and trim figure, while Holly sat patiently in line for some of the attention that was being dished out.

Unfortunately, once people tore themselves away from the splendid spaniel, they turned to Holly with a look of disgust and walked away, leaving poor Holly looking perplexed and waiting for cuddles as everyone left.

CHAPTER NINE
Rehab

Holly's weight loss and transformation didn't just happen; we both put a lot of work in to get the results we needed. After her initial weigh in at the vets, we had to attend 'Doggy Weightwatchers' every week for Holly to be weighed and measured to monitor her progress. Some weeks I'd thought she'd lose a lot more than she did – being on a high fibre diet she would regularly pooh her body weight three times a day! I used to laugh at the dog owners that walked around with tiny little poop bags. I needed bags the size of bin liners for Holly's offerings.

The vet we had enrolled with had moved to new premises and just built a wonderful new Canine Rehabilitation Centre that hosted a large hydrotherapy pool, an underwater treadmill, and they had excellent physiotherapists on hand if required. Holly really did have the very best of Private Health Care. With her own team of Private Carers, Her Ladyship got treatment fit for a Queen. She became a very spoilt and pampered patient as she was nursed back to health.

She had regular sessions on the underwater treadmill which was exactly as it sounds. Just like a normal treadmill in the gym, but surrounded by glass like a giant fish tank. Holly would wear the equivalent of a life jacket – the largest size available to get round her big tummy – and then the tank would fill with water up to Holly's back as she waited for the treadmill to start moving.

Everything was very slow and gentle to begin with but as her fitness levels improved, she was able to have longer and faster sessions. The water and the exercise would aid her weight loss and help build up her muscles and her leg strength.

I could never be certain what Holly made of all of this as she was so placid and just seemed to take whatever was thrown at her. As soon as I was charged with Holly's care and from the minute I was solely responsible for her health and wellbeing, I worried constantly. Holly was so dependent on me to make the right decisions for her and she had already been through so much. More than anything, I wanted her to be happy in her new home and not feel like she'd just come to yet another house where existence had to be endured. However, I had to be guided by the vets and there was no doubt that Holly's rotund condition had to be addressed or the alternative outcome would not be a happy one.

Holly at Aqua Aerobics

After tentative beginnings, Holly began to love her treadmill sessions. She used to try and catch the toys bobbing around in the water, and then looked decidedly disgruntled when they bobbed out of her reach and she ended up splashed in the face. After the session was finished and her buoyancy jacket was removed, she got her much loved rub down with a towel. This obviously reminded her of 'morning cuddles' and she was beside herself with glee and very often ran her nurse a merry dance as she tried to dry her patient.

Our visits to this wonderful facility became a regular occurrence and Holly's and my routine together continued to develop. We began to live in our own little world, with our own vocabulary and I often caught myself saying to friends and family – 'I have to take Holly to Aqua Aerobics' or 'Holly's due in Rehab that day', much to everyone's amusement and very often, confusion

As the months passed, I wanted to continue fundraising for some of my much loved bear charities. The summer of 2009 saw Animals Asia, who do incredible work to free Asiatic Black Bears from the brutal bear farming industry in Asia, holding a sponsored walk in Holyrood Park in Edinburgh. Brilliant, I thought, this is something Holly and I can do together. It would be good for both of us. We would only do a really short walk so as not to push Holly too much and after getting the go ahead from the vet, we started to get people to sponsor us and do our bit to help advertise the walk locally.

I still had a number of contacts in the local media from my years working for WSPA, so I got in touch with them. Having a rough idea of what makes a 'good story', I sent off an email explaining Holly's story, the progress we'd made over the last few months and how we now wanted to help raise money together to support efforts to end bear farming. The press loved it and the phone started ringing.

Holly had captured so many hearts already and she knew it. As she started to feel better, her cheeky nature began to emerge and she knew exactly how to beguile everyone. She already had all the staff at the vets wrapped around her little paw and treating her like a Princess and she had me on a string and at her constant beck and call. She had also captured the hearts of the neighbours and knew exactly which houses she'd get a biscuit at and lingered a little longer outside their doors waiting for a treat to be brought out to her and now, she was going to be a media star too. Perhaps I should start thinking about getting her an agent!

We were contacted by five local papers and once the articles began to appear, Holly even got a mention on the Steve Wright show on BBC Radio 2. The headlines seemed to capture everyone's attention 'Portly Pooch pounds the pavements', 'Hefty Holly sheds two stone to help the bears' and 'Ten stone dog finds new leash of life.' She even had her own Just Giving Page. She would be impossible to live with soon if fame went to her head.

I have fond memories of one of my four legged celebrity's photo shoots when two photographers from different papers arrived at the same time. We'd both smartened ourselves up a little; Holly had had a good brush and wore her pink 'Princess' collar with pride. I wore a satin type blouse with dress trousers and slapped on a bit of lipstick. I had recently had my patio done and I had hoped the photos would be taken there as it was a sea of colour, with all the new plants in bloom and although a bit windy, it was a lovely sunny day.

Alas no. They insisted on traipsing off to the

overgrown, dandelion strewn fields at the back of our estate. I looked at Holly and she looked at me and I whispered 'we'll do it for the bears.'

One of the photographers had designed a makeshift 'Sponsor me' sign with a bit of A4 paper and some thread to hang around Holly's neck. She asked me to get Holly to sit down. I had to stand over her with a leg on either side, holding her collar with one hand to stop her bolting off to see the other dogs strolling nearby all while holding the sign down to stop the wind blowing it with the other hand. As if that wasn't enough, she then told me to keep my hair out of my eyes – how many hands did she think I had?!

Next, the second photographer wanted me to kneel down beside Holly so we were face to face. By this time Holly was getting thoroughly fed up and bearing in mind, this was our local field where everyone walked their dogs to relieve their bowels and bladders, I was none too enamoured myself with the thought of having to kneel beside her. By this point, however, I think we were both willing to do anything to get it over and done with. So there we were, Holly sitting with a sign round her neck and me lying on the ground beside her in a poop riddled field, looking like I was dressed for dinner.

Thankfully, that was the last photo shoot and we could both get back to concentrating on the matter in hand, training for the walk.

The day of the walk arrived and armed with bottles of water and Holly's bowl, I said to her, 'Just do what you can manage, as soon as you get too tired, we'll stop.' I was so proud of my dog, who never ceased to amaze me with her fighting spirit and determination, when she set off enthusiastically with the other dog walkers. Holly always liked to be in charge so, occasionally, she barked her orders at the other dogs, keeping everyone in line. Some of the fitter and healthier dogs went on the much longer route but Holly and I stuck to the shorter distance, perfect for special needs doggies.

She did brilliantly and raised a massive £600. She managed about two miles, so I think that must have been around fourteen miles in doggy distance. She had earned a well-deserved rest and we headed home so she could put her paws up for a while before her next fundraiser.

It was a lovely day and a real sign of Holly's remarkable progress.

Paws for a rest

CHAPTER TEN
Power Shift

Holly and I settled into a great routine and her transformation had begun to be noticed by everyone who knew her and dog walkers who didn't but had watched her change from a sad, miserable, sorry looking soul to a much happier, lither dog. So many people commented on how lucky she was to have me but in my heart, I knew it was always the other way round.

Holly had been so good for me in such a short period of time. She had brought the first rays of sunshine for years and she gave renewed meaning and purpose to my life. She managed very early on, I'm sure through her special brand of dog telepathy, to let me know that if she wasn't going to get an extra biscuit, I certainly wasn't going to be allowed a bag of crisps or an extra piece of chocolate. She would stare unflinchingly at me if I dared to try. Her guilt trip very quickly made me feel that if she was going to have to go on a strict diet and exercise regime, then so was I.

Therefore, I bought some cook books on healthy eating and got myself a personal trainer. I nicknamed him Tarzan. He put me through so many gruelling workouts at the gym which I groaned and moaned my way through, I think if he'd told me to 'embrace the pain' one more time, I would have embraced the heaviest dumbbell I could have lifted and dropped it on his toe!

However, my and my canine team member's joint efforts paid off and in those early months and years, we both lost around three stone and enjoyed our new leases of life together. As my fitness and state of mind improved, I decided to get off the antidepressants that I had been taking since my redundancy. In a way, I felt it was my last link to those years that had been so unhappy for so long. Holly and I were slowly but surely mending each other.

My driving school business continued to thrive giving me a little more structure and security but the cancellations were very hard to cope with. These could happen at any time and with very short notice, making it almost impossible to budget or save and as someone who was very used to working hard and long hours, I was often left with days that could feel very disjointed and piecemeal, leaving me feeling uneasy and frustrated. This situation was only eased partially with the introduction of a lesson cancellation policy, which I often felt wasn't even worth the paper it was written on – if my pupils didn't have any money, I could hardly march them to the cash machine. I pretty quickly had to harden up in this connection and if I was messed around too many times, I would have to drop that pupil and replace them with one I could rely on.

On the roads, it wasn't my pupils that caused me stress, but far more often, other qualified road users who had clearly forgotten that no-one was born driving and they were learners once upon a time too. Driving aggressively behind a learner won't get anyone where they're going any quicker and can be enough to put a learner off for life. I certainly had to learn a whole new set of people skills as a driving instructor and a lot of patience in many different situations, but my confidence grew as time went on and it was a job that certainly kept my mind alert and focused. Although it had its difficulties, the income from the job allowed me to work a four-day week and gave me the flexible hours I needed to come home throughout each day at regular intervals to check how Holly was and give her medicine as and when it was required. She had to have three small meals a day to keep her metabolism going, so only a job with flexible hours would allow me to care for Holly as necessary.

It was such a delight watching Holly's transformation and watching her true character emerge, one that had previously been so beaten into submission through excess weight, ill health and neglect. Somewhere along our journey together, the roles shifted and she became the Boss. She was no longer my dog, I was her Human. She loved her new home and I just happened to live there too. She always managed to tell me what she wanted and when she wanted it. As she knew I was putty in her paws, she usually got her own way. She was extremely spoilt. Her favourite place in the whole house remained her sofa, well both of them actually – reclining ones at that. Nothing but the best for Holly! Ever since the very first day that she came to live with me, when she had shown her sheer determination to get up onto the sofa beside me, it had become her favourite spot. When we had guests, if one of them was sitting on the sofa, Holly would very surreptitiously get up beside them and then gently but slyly push her way in behind their back until she'd managed to push them off. As she was still a large dog, if she decided to spread out, there really wasn't a lot of room for anyone else. Luckily, all my friends were animal lovers and saw the comical side as we very often ended up sitting on the floor, while Holly lay reclining on her thrown, surveying her subjects beneath her. Given what she had been through and loving seeing her cheeky and comical side emerging, it was always so hard to give her a row. When she was particularly naughty and demanding, I used to try and look at her firmly and say in a stern voice 'it's just as well you came to live with me as no-one else would put up with your nonsense!' It was always a pointless reprimand, as she would just look at me with her big brown eyes and sit wagging her tail.

One of her other favourite tricks was to sit spread out on her sofa, with one arm on the armrest, the other by her side, hind legs stretched out as though she was on a chaise longue waiting to be fed grapes and champagne.

Holly awaiting her servants

From her position of great comfort, she would stare at me, sitting on the other sofa across the room. She would then start with a small whine that would gradually get louder and louder and escalate into a bark if I didn't go over immediately to give her a cuddle. I have no doubt the dog behaviourists will be having heart attacks and bursting to point out all the mistakes I made with Holly, but when you have nursed a dog back from such ill health, knowing each extra day with them is one you may not have had, it is very hard not to shower them with love.

Holly had claimed the couch as her own to such an extent that if I left the room for a few minutes, I would often return to find she had pinched my seat. I eventually got wise to this and thought I'd managed to outsmart her one day. I had a lot of work to do and I'd been sitting on the couch by the window. This was another of Holly's favourite spots as she could monitor and supervise anything going on outside and bark at any other dog who dared walk past her Castle and threaten her rule. I had my laptop and my papers laid out just as I needed them to continue my work, so when I decided to go and make a cup of coffee, I thought I'd found the perfect way to get one up on her to keep my seat safe and play her at her own game.

Therefore, I put my briefcase on my seat and told Holly to stay where she was and I would be back in a minute. I returned from the kitchen with my coffee, only to find Madam sitting **on top** of the briefcase staring out of the window. My plan had failed miserably. You had to give her full marks for determination and perseverance. She was most definitely the Boss and yes, I know, I let her get away with it.

Holly on the Job

As her weight loss continued, she became a lot lighter on her feet and more agile and with it came an increase in the incidents of food theft. If I gave her an inch, she took a mile and when previously she had never been able to move quickly enough to steal food, now she was a lot faster on her feet and would regularly swipe treats off a plate before anyone could stop her. One day I was sitting on the couch, eating my tea. I'd made a vegetable curry and had a piece of naan bread resting on the side of my plate. All of a sudden, like a shark emerging from the depths of the ocean to devour a treat on the surface, a big black wet nose and big brown eyes appeared from under the plate and my naan bread disappeared in a flash. Again, this behaviour came with such mixed feelings for me. The first time I caught Holly with her front paws up on the kitchen work surface, balancing gingerly on her back legs, looking to see what tasty morsels had been left out for her, I didn't know whether to give her a row or praise her for managing to get her front paws off the floor.

I will never forget the day I came home from work to find the contents of the fridge strewn out over the kitchen floor and Holly paw deep in a variety of goodies with a very guilty look on her face. Needless to say, the pursuing row and ticking off had little effect on her and she just ended up looking very pleased with herself.

However, the strange thing was that the evidence at the scene of the crime didn't really add up. The inside of the fridge was soaking and a bottle of sparkling water in the door was split. On further investigation, it dawned on me that I think it was actually my fault all along. The evening before, I'd had friends round and I'd put a bottle of sparking water in the freezer to chill and stupidly forgot to take it out. The next day, I removed it, completely frozen and put it in the fridge to defrost while I was at work. However, I think what must have happened was when it melted the top blew off and the bottle split, hence the fridge door flying open along with its contents. So although it wasn't actually Holly's fault, she certainly took full advantage of the situation.

I did feel awful about falsely accusing her, but in my defence she was the prime suspect at the scene of the crime, with a history of misdemeanours to her name and looking very guilty, so you can understand the miscarriage of justice on this occasion.

When Holly had originally been put on her prescription dog food diet, she was given a special tag for her collar which read 'Please do not feed me, I'm on a special diet.'

After her latest spate of food thefts and after much debate with Holly about her behaviour, we decided we'd change it to read 'Please do not feed me, I'll help myself.'

HOLLY, THE MAHOGANY GIRL

CHAPTER ELEVEN
Be Careful What You Wish For

The summer after our sponsored walk, Holly and I decided to take a well-deserved holiday or as Holly preferred 'Hollyday'.

As I'd been finding my feet again work-wise, I had also been pursuing my love of writing and had been commissioned to write a few pieces by a magazine that specialised on articles about Scottish Islands. One of my incredibly inspirational friends had, a few years earlier, packed up her home and successful business in Edinburgh to move lock, stock and barrel to the little island of Easdale on the West Coast of Scotland. She lived in a caravan for over three years while she built her own house and then she went on to buy and regenerate the island's pub and restaurant. She was a truly remarkable woman. I'd already done a story on her initial move to the island and had been asked to do a follow-up a year on, which would also incorporate the stories of some of the other islanders.

Easdale is the smallest permanently inhabited island of the Inner Hebrides with around seventy residents and is situated approximately sixteen miles south of Oban. It has no roads, so is a completely car free island and the main mode of transport is a wheelbarrow. It is accessed by a small passenger ferry from the mainland. I turned to Holly as she sat beside me on the couch one afternoon and said 'Do you fancy going on a little boat girl? Maybe we could borrow your life jacket from Aqua Aerobics.' As far as I knew, she'd never been on a boat, come to think of it, I had no way of knowing if she'd ever had any holidays before.

So the next month, we headed off to Easdale so that I could do my follow-up interviews. It was a bit of an interesting challenge getting Holly, my bags, and her bedding and food onto the little ferry as it bobbed about in the harbour, bouncing off the pier and it was nothing short of a miracle that neither of us ended up in the water. Once safely on board, we hung on tightly as the little boat sped off to the island. We had a lovely few days on Easdale and as usual, Holly made herself the centre of attention. We had also booked a couple of days in a log cabin in Killin on the way home and although we both loved Easdale, we arrived at the cabin eaten alive by midges. I have always loved the West Coast of Scotland and would live there if it wasn't for the pesky Scottish midges. Holly seemed to enjoy her trip to the island – I was opening her up to new experiences and we were making memories to treasure. I certainly would anyway.

When we arrived at the log cabin and continued to enjoy our first holiday together, I quickly realised this set up was perfect and we would go on to have a number of log cabin breaks together. The cabins were all on one level and although Holly wasn't allowed in the bedrooms, she was at least on the same level as me. For all the bravado she was beginning to exhibit, she could still show signs of being very insecure and would often look to me for reassurance in unfamiliar situations. Although I loved having Holly on the couch at home, I have never really been a great lover of dogs on my bed. In the beginning and because of her size, Holly very rarely attempted to come up the stairs at home. When she did attempt the climb, I have no idea what technique she used. I used to lie in bed and listen to her making her way up each step – she sounded like she had about a hundred and five legs! On the rare occasions that she did came upstairs, as usual, I very quickly gave in to her pleas to come up on the bed and, indeed, I helped her – no wonder she never did as she was told! Again, we developed a routine that was a finely tuned joint effort to achieve her end goal of being able to take up three quarters of the bed while I dangled off the remaining quarter. Our modus operandi involved Holly once again getting her front paws up on the bed, while I heaved up her back end, a technique that had served us well in the past in various situations. This worked really well until the night, half way through this procedure, when her head came up just as mine moved down and we had a major collision. I just about split my chin open and put my teeth through my lip and Holly must have had one almighty headache. After that, we reached a tacit, mutual understanding that we probably wouldn't attempt that particular manoeuvre again.

In our years together, we would have a number of log cabin breaks and Holly was very settled sleeping at the bedroom door keeping an eye on me and guarding the cabin. Being a woman travelling alone, having Holly with me always made me feel very safe. We really were a great team.

There was only one trip we went on, where I would feel real fear.

Much as I'd loved my previous trips to the Slate Islands as they were known – Easdale, Seil and Luing - the weather had been glorious each time, the ferry crossings calm and peaceful and the only testing times were brought on by the summer midges. I wanted to do a winter trip so that I would hopefully get the chance to experience true wild winter island life so the next time we planned a trip in November.

As Easdale and Luing were 'true' islands that had to be reached by boat, if the weather was bad there was a real chance the ferries would be off and we wouldn't be able to reach our destination. It would end up being a wasted journey from Edinburgh. Therefore, I decided to book accommodation on the Isle of Seil.

The Isle of Seil is situated twelve miles south of Oban and is connected to the mainland of Argyll by the Clachan Bridge – also known as 'The Bridge over the

Atlantic Ocean'. The bridge was built in 1792 by John Stevenson for the sum of £450. Legend had it that on completion, a horse pulling a cartload of hay was sent across the bridge to test its strength. There is much debate as to whether or not Seil should be counted as an island at all because of the fixed link to the mainland. Just over the bridge is the Tigh an Truish Inn which means 'House of Trousers'. The name comes from the time after the 1745 rebellion when kilts were banned and it was the place where islanders, heading for the mainland, had to swap their kilts for trousers.

After searching the internet for self-catering accommodation, I booked a lovely little cottage. It wasn't ideal as it was on two floors, but there was a limited choice. I could see from their website that the main bedroom had a lovely big skylight window right above the bed and I thought how perfect it would be to lie gazing up at the stars. It would be the ideal location as I would still be able to get there by car, even if the ferries were off. If they weren't, Holly and I would still be able to get over to Easdale to see our friends.

As the weather forecast emerged for the week of our break, I began to commend myself on my foresight as my wish for a wild weather trip looked like it may come true and I may at last get to witness the islands' wild side and their vulnerability at the hands of nature. However, as the weather forecast predicted torrential rain and gale force winds, the novice island hopper in me started to get a little edgy. I turned to Holly, as we were watching the forecast on TV and said 'Don't worry, we've planned for this. We'll still get to our cottage and it will be an exciting adventure for us.' It then crossed my mind that perhaps this time, I should take a rubber ring and some armbands for her just in case we got thrown overboard. If I was going to subject her to a choppy ferry ride, the least I could do was ensure her safety.

The journey over to Seil was indeed in torrential rain and gusting winds. Driving along the exposed narrow roads in the Scottish Highlands, there were times it felt like the car was in a washing machine. The rain was still pelting down on arrival at our beautiful cosy cottage so we got the car unpacked as quickly as possible and settled in for the evening. It was a beautiful, well-equipped cottage and the owners had very thoughtfully left out a welcome tray with tea and scones. It was lovely to be warm and dry after the long and wild journey up.

Having been on the road since late morning, we decided to get an early night. I wanted Holly in the bedroom with me as she never settled if I was far away or out of her sight and we'd brought her giant Scooby Doo beanbag bed, which of course was never used at home as Her Ladyship far preferred the comfort of her sofa, but it would be a perfect bed for her here.

I settled Holly on her bed and climbed into mine. As I lay tired and relaxed gazing at the night sky, I drifted off to sleep with my travelling companion snoozing contentedly on the floor beside me.

Then it happened. The most horrendous thunderstorm I'd ever experienced in my life bolted me out of my slumber. It sounded like bombs and sticks of dynamite were going off in unison. The lightning was ferocious and yet captivating, right up until the point I was looking up at the window and there was one almighty flash and I could feel the pain in my eyes. The torrential rain and hail were pelting so hard against the window, I thought it was going to collapse inwards with a howling, merciless gale right behind it. It didn't help that the window had started to leak too. I was frozen with equal amounts of fear and awe at the force of nature.

My imagination often runs riot in situations like this and within minutes, turns a slightly testing situation into a major disaster. As the intensity of the lightning increased and the bolts crackled and flashed across the night sky my mind ran riot. I was already envisaging it striking the TV aerial and starting a fire downstairs which would trap Holly and I in the upstairs bedroom. The room only had a small side window and the Velux window up onto the roof.

I played out the scenario in my head of the fire ripping through the house and up to the second floor, the smoke billowing through underneath the door and the flames devouring the door itself, completely trapping us. How on earth would I get Holly out? There's no way she or I for that matter would fit through the side window and not a hope in hell that I could lift Holly up through the skylight and onto the roof. Despite my extra weight lifting sessions at the gym, I could rarely lift anything heavier than a cotton bud above my head, so that escape route was doomed.

As I lay frozen with fear in my bed with my duvet clutched tightly beneath my chin, while the storm raged around me, I remember someone saying that dogs always pick up on your emotions and can sense your fear. I was so worried that if Holly saw how frightened I was, she would become really distressed too. Fighting my terror, with a shaky voice, I tried desperately to reassure her, like a parent comforting their frightened child 'It's ok baby, everything's alright. Good girl Holly, mummy will look after you.'

Then came yet another earth shattering noise to add to the deafening thunderclaps…Holly… SNORING! I had been so gripped by fear and paralysed by the disastrous fire scenario and the dilemma of working out our escape route that I was oblivious to the fact that Holly was completely unperturbed by the brutal storm. She had snored her way through the whole thing, untroubled and with not so much as a flicker of her eyelids. And to think, with it being November, I had been worried how she would cope with fireworks night when we got home!

According to the islanders the next day, it had been one of the most severe storms they had had in years.

I made a mental note to myself for the future…be careful what you wish for.

CHAPTER TWELVE
Stalking Wildebeest

Holly and I had five winters together and two of them were the worst winters Scotland had seen for nearly one hundred years. With temperatures falling as low as minus 22C and biting winds that would not have been amiss in the Arctic our daily walks became short and sweet not least because it took us both all our time to stay upright. The roads and pavements were like ice rinks and snowdrifts were waist high. Anytime Holly squatted to relieve herself she got a very cold bottom and her usual habit of sticking her head in a bush while she emptied her bladder would result in her having a pile of snow falling on her head. It was a really comical habit she'd developed from quite early on. I could only liken it to a child thinking if they covered their eyes, no-one could see them – perhaps Holly thought if she hid her head in a bush she would have privacy while going to the lavatory – she was a classy lady after all.

Holly protecting her modesty while attending to business

Without fail, one or other of us would slip and fall on our winter walks. If it wasn't Holly doing her best impression of Bambi on the ice it was me spending most of our walks on my backside. I was certain that one of us would throw a hip sooner or later and I was pretty sure it wouldn't be Holly. After grumbling one night to my mother about how utterly freezing these walks were, she lent me one of her lovely cosy winter hats. From that point on, without exception, every time I wore her hat, I fell over. I was convinced mum was playing a trick on me and had somehow loaded the hat with a weight of some sort!

Holly loved to walk along with her nose to the ground as if she was shovelling the snow up with her snout. She also loved to eat the snow too, she really was now getting such great pleasure from life. If our harsh winters had continued much longer, I worried she may have had an identity crisis as many times she would go out a black dog and come in a white one.

One of the sweetest things I ever watched her do happened one night after we returned from our evening walk during the first bout of heavy snow we had together. I had no idea if she had ever even seen snow before as our winters up until that point had been really mild.

The snow continued to fall heavily after we got home so I let her out in the garden to watch her reaction. She stood perfectly still in the middle of the snow covered lawn and looked up into the night sky as the falling snow flakes landed one by one on the tip of her nose and suddenly, with no warning, she started leaping and bounding ecstatically around the garden, resembling a cross between a rabbit and a kangaroo; it was so wonderful to watch.

The docile lumbering dog that had staggered across my font lawn only to slump down on my living room floor when she arrived in June 2008 was now propelling her way around the back garden like a whirlwind as if for the first time, she suddenly knew what it was like to enjoy life at long last.

For the most part, Holly and I loved our walks together apart from on one occasion when Madam right royally disgraced herself to such an extent that we had a serious falling out. Before they built hundreds of houses, the area we lived was surrounded by lovely big fields and we were spoilt for choice when it came to walks. Our freezing cold winters brought some of the brightest, crispest days with the golden sun lighting up the bluest of cloud free skies, making the snow glisten like fields of sparkling diamonds. These were always my most favourite days. Holly and I wrapped up warm and cosy and headed off for our morning walk. It was a truly beautiful day and my companion and I set off with a spring in our step, feeling really good.

Once we reached the field, I let Holly off the lead. Away she trotted with a little hop, skip and a jump of enthusiasm as her lighter frame now allowed, contentedly sniffing all the new smells around her. Actually, Holly didn't really 'sniff' as such but more accurately behaved like she was snorting for truffles, nose glued to the ground.

We always followed the well-trodden paths but it was such a beautiful day and the walk was so enjoyable, I decided to go a little further afield and off the beaten track. BIG mistake!

Holly lagged behind a little at one point, spending a long time sniffing something of great interest to her. Then, with dismay, I saw it, the focus of her undivided attention. A great big pile of steaming hot fox pooh.

Like car crash television, before my very eyes and with my feet unable to run fast enough to stop her, she launched herself at the offensive pile head first, like a polar bear bursting through the ice for tasty morsels below. She started sliding around, rubbing her head, neck and ears, coating her fur in the stench like she was wallowing in sweet smelling candyfloss. The horror of the situation dawned on me as I finally reached the pongy pooch to find even her chain link collar covered in the green and brown stinking mess. I had no alternative but to try and pull her away, but despite her weight loss she remained a very big dog and her size made parental control rather difficult at times and even more frustrating in such a 'rolling in fox pooh' emergency. It was a highly traumatic incident – for me anyway!

On arriving home she was promptly marched out into the back garden to be hosed down. I can barely write about it as just recalling the whole incident makes me feel nauseous! She was bathed and bathed, dried with the hairdryer, then smothered in scented talc and brushed and brushed and yet still, she stank.

I phoned Holly's 'Beauty Parlour' where she had been for a pamper session a few times in the early days to help her dry skin and asked the dog groomer what I should do. She suggested wiping vinegar and warm water on her and online, they suggested tomato ketchup to mask the smell. So I had the choice of Holly smelling like a hotdog or a bag of chips, but anything was better than the rank smell of fox pooh, so I chose the bag of chips.

What a relief when the vinegar began to mask the smell, but sadly it was short lived. All too soon the rancid odour began to permeate through the vinegar. The paint on the walls started blistering, the paper started peeling, the windows started cracking and my eyes were watering and bloodshot. Okay, perhaps I'm exaggerating a little but I have to adequately portray the extent of my suffering after Her Ladyship's revolting indulgence!

The smell lingered for a good few days, despite more vinegar, talcum powder and baby wipes. The only thing that got rid of it completely was another visit to Holly's salon for a shampoo and blow dry before she returned to her full glory.

The experience and smell was so awful, I could not understand why dogs got so much pleasure from doing this. My old dog Tulsa used to love to roll in cow pats, so I knew it wasn't just Holly, so I turned to the internet for an explanation of this very socially unacceptable doggie habit.

Apparently, it is a trait handed down from their ancestors. The dogs roll in the offensive substance to disguise their own scent. This enables them to 'blend' into their environment while they are stalking their prey.

The incident was followed by my having a long chat with Holly, I talked, and she had no choice but to listen. I politely informed her that I'm sure this behaviour would be very useful when she was next stalking a herd of Wildebeest in the Serengeti, but until then, she had a nice tasty bowl of dog food at home waiting for her and she wasn't going to need to stalk anything anytime soon!

CHAPTER THIRTEEN
Fetch

The winter gave way to a lovely spring and summer and Holly continued to thrive. Even after her weight loss, I always felt she was very large for a bitch. I knew Labradors could come in a variety of shapes and sizes but I always thought she was closer to the size of a male Labrador than a female.

However, considering where she'd come from, Holly's size and weight never really fitted into 'normal' parameters. She now weighed around 39kg and had lost a massive 23kg – nearly four stone and almost half her original weight. She was amazing and I was so proud of her. She loved life, she loved playing, she loved people and most of all she now loved cuddles.

The socially inept dog that I had met what felt like a lifetime ago, that had no idea how to react to affection, now couldn't get enough love, embraces and interaction. Walks that had previously been an unbearable hardship and test of endurance had now become the highlight of her day.

However, Holly seemed to have missed out on the basics of puppyhood and never showed as much interest in toys as you would expect from a Labrador or indeed the simple pleasures of chasing a ball or fetching a stick.

Therefore, one lovely summer's day, my mother and I decided to pack a picnic, go for a lovely country walk with one of Holly's balls and try to teach her the art of 'fetch.'

We arrived at our picnic site and put all our bags down on the bench. Then Mum, Holly and I lined up in a row in preparation for me throwing the ball. I said to Holly, 'Granny and I will show you how it's done and all three of us can run for the ball and have a little competition to see who reaches it first' - why on earth I thought she'd understand this, I don't know. Knowing Holly, she probably understood perfectly well but thought, that's far too much like hard work.

So with the three of us standing in a row, I hurled the ball as far as I could. Mum and I shot off as fast as two people in their mid-forties and early eighties could after the ball, eagerly anticipating Holly following us enthusiastically. As we bounded forwards as fast as we could following the ball, we suddenly realised there was no sign of Holly.

As we had lined up, thrown the ball and darted forward trying to teach our pupil the art of fetch she had promptly turned around, hotfooted it back in the opposite direction and made her way back to the picnic and was merrily tucking in to her own private feast as she watched mum and I running off into the distance, chasing her ball and doing all the hard work while she enjoyed a snack and watched the entertainment.

It really was one of the funniest things. It would have provided great amusement to anyone who happened to be watching.

It was and still is a lovely memory, in fact one of my fondest and one I like to hang on to, as things were about to change and Holly was about to have to face yet another battle.

HOLLY, THE MAHOGANY GIRL

CHAPTER FOURTEEN
Hormones and Rear Ends

When Holly came to live with me, I thought the main problem I would have to address was her weight. The only other issue was that she had not been spayed and this can also lead to other risks in a female dog such as pyometra, a uterine infection that can prove fatal, so the priority after her weight loss was always going to be getting her spayed. However, any operation at her size carried far too high a risk if it involved a general anaesthetic. So the original plan was, without further delay, to get the weight off her, get her fit and well, and then take it from there. If I'm honest, the thought of having her spayed terrified me from the moment it was mentioned.

Although an extremely common operation, it was a big operation and I couldn't bear the thought of Holly having to go through more than she absolutely had to.

When I tried to imagine things from her point of view, there were times I thought, she must really hate me.

Not only had she been through all the problems of her former life, but since she came to live with me, she'd been subjected to walks in all weather when she just wanted to laze around the house, she'd been given a diet of boring dry dog food when she'd been used to pizza, she'd had her big tummy strapped into a lifejacket and was made to walk on an underwater treadmill in the doggy gym, and she'd actually been expected to over exert herself by chasing balls! All very undignified behaviour for a lady who was born to live on the couch. I hope she realised that I'd done it all for her, to make her as happy and healthy as possible and I was always driven by what was in her best interests. Still, I couldn't help but feel at times, she must think I was Attila the Hun.

Despite being an unspayed bitch, Holly was never messy. Having never had a female dog, I was unsure of what to expect if and when she went into season. I think on one occasion, there had been a tiny spot of blood on one of her blankets, but really that was it in all the years I had her. I think her entire body had ground to a halt with her weight increase and never really functioned properly. Although there were no physical signs of her being an 'intact' female, there were definitely behavioural signs.

Although from very early on, Holly had dictated that the couch would be her bed, my friend had kindly bought her a great big Scooby Doo beanbag bed, so that Holly could always feel she had a place that was 'just hers' and she could rest and retreat there whenever she needed her own space. Fat chance of that! As usual, Holly had her own ideas and nothing would keep her from her beloved couch. Only on the very rare occasion would she sleep on the beanbag and that was usually if we were on holiday – despite equal determination to make any couch in our holiday accommodation hers too. However, in Holly's eyes, Scooby came in very useful in other ways.

Again, from fairly early on, Holly began to exhibit one of her more comical behaviours, albeit a rather embarrassing trait and one that could cause great chaos. Holly's hormones very often got the better of her. There seemed to be no rhyme or reason as to when this would happen and no pattern. Initially, Holly would try to squeeze into the tiniest spot in the house or become fixated with a certain part of the carpet, usually in the hardest possible place to reach and try to dig it up.

This would be really frantic behaviour and nothing would stop her. It was alarming for me as I couldn't tell if she was distressed or not or just displaying some natural instinct to dig. If there happened to be a pile of magazines or a piece of furniture in the way, they would immediately be scattered or pushed out of the way as Holly forced her way in to her chosen spot. She wasn't being naughty, she had never been a destructive dog, she was simply being completely driven by her hormones. Again, I tried to research this behaviour and after talking it through with the vet, we thought she may be having phantom pregnancies and 'nesting'. It could be hard to watch at times as she seemed so agitated. It may have been something triggered by a memory from her past and

I just didn't know how to help her. All I could do was to try to comfort and reassure her until the moment passed.

There were times when it also provided great amusement and she would have me and anyone else who happened to witness her socially questionable behaviour in fits of giggles. It was especially comical when she was bigger as there was little option but to take cover and get out of her way when she was on the move and on a mission.

As she squeezed her bulk under the smallest of the nest of tables to dig up her chosen part of the carpet, on more than one occasion, when she was finished, she would end up wandering around the living-room with a table on her back. Then poor Scooby would be on the receiving end of Madam's unwanted affections and become the object of her hormonal desires. On regular occasions the Scooby bean bag would be dragged from the living room to the kitchen and back again, in Holly's clutches as she enthusiastically gave him the once over, administering her affections and sending everything in her path flying in the process. I thought this not so pleasant doggy trait was only exhibited by male dogs but again, after discussion with the vet, he told me it's quite common in unspayed bitches and that I was to try not to worry as Holly was probably having the time of her life.

So it was another aspect of 'Life with Holly' that we adjusted to and we learnt to batten down the hatches and get out of the way whenever these episodes occurred. I'm afraid poor Scooby never got off so lightly.

On one of our lovely walks together on a beautiful sunny day, I marvelled at how fantastically gorgeous my lovely brave Holly was looking. We'd come a long way together. We had completely transformed each other's lives. The significance of each of us to the other was unquestionable. She looked slim-ish, fit and well and her coat was thick and lustrous and gleamed and shone in the sun, a clear sign of the improvements in her health.

When Holly arrived, her fur was very dull and sparse. You could see her skin through her thin patchy coat. When her thyroid issues were addressed and her diet improved, so did her coat and as she moulted, it grew back in thicker and glossier than ever, it was almost like a puppy's fur, it was so soft and fluffy.

Through her many visits to Doggy Weightwatchers and Aqua Aerobics in Rehab, she had become a much loved patient at the Veterinary Surgery. When it became clear how often she would need to be seen and monitored, since there were a number of vets in the practice, I asked if she could be seen by the same one each time so we had some consistency and continuity and throughout Holly's care, I would be reassured that the vet treating her would be fully aware of her complex medical history. I will never be able to thank the vet enough, who cared for her throughout her life and he would be with us to the end.

I remember on one visit, we gave him a terrible fright. He had always marvelled at Holly's thick gleaming coat and was completely shocked at one of our visits while Holly was moulting. When she went through this process her coat reverted to being dull and course. Her skin would become extremely flaky and she would look like she was covered in dandruff or worse, had mites.

When the vet saw us he exclaimed with great concern, 'What on earth's happened?!' I replied, 'Oh don't worry, this is completely normal Holly behaviour.' I then explained that when Holly went through this process, she was like a caterpillar shedding its skin and metamorphosing into a butterfly. In a few days, Holly would once again, be sporting her trademark shiny coat. Being a Lady of high standards, I liked to think this was Holly getting rid of her Winter Wardrobe and bringing in her new Spring Ensemble. It was almost indicative of her overall transformation over the years.

As Holly became a regular visitor to the vets, she again, captured hearts and became very spoilt. To be honest, I think she ended up with her own little Harem, her personal team of Veterinary Health Care Professionals at her beck and call, as she wrapped everyone round her little paw. The team there were wise to Holly's favourite game of going through people's legs to get her bottom rubbed and she just loved it when everyone played along.

As Holly's health improved and her energy returned, she also found her voice and had become a bit of a barker at times. Used to getting her own way and being the centre of attention, I always worried a little that she may give them a hard time anytime she had to go in as a day patient – it was a very busy practice, there were of course, other animals to be looked after. Holly couldn't expect *all* the attention, *all* the time like she got at home.

One day I asked her vet how she was after I dropped her off - it was always much harder for me leaving her than it was for her staying, as apparently she was so pampered she had a great time while I was left at home biting my fingernails down to the knuckle, worrying about her. It was the vet that we'd asked to be assigned to and he knew her very well and as with most people who met her, had become very fond of her. He reported that on most occasions she was fine, but there was one time that he was tending to another dog directly opposite Holly and she started barking at him and he couldn't really understand why. I replied, 'Oh that's easy. You're HER vet now - that means in Holly's head, she expects you to give her your undivided attention at all times.'

Although never able to know what the future may bring, I did feel fairly confident that when I took Holly on, the major issue we would have to deal with was her weight and once her thyroid was under control and she began to shed the pounds, I thought we were home and dry and could enjoy a long, happy and healthy life together.

However, one week in September 2010, I had to face the horrendous situation of *having* to get Holly operated on. Having been told on many occasions of the pretty major risk she would face being anaesthetised to be spayed and to now face a situation where she couldn't avoid having a procedure, sent my heart plummeting to my boots. Holly had become rather preoccupied with her bottom. Since dogs always seem to have a fascination with their rear ends, I didn't really think much of it. However, very suddenly a large, red and swollen abscess type lump appeared on her bottom so I took her straight down to the vets as soon as I could get an appointment. The vet took one look at it and told me to bring her in first thing in the morning, so that they could operate on her. I was so worried. Holly had become such a massive part of my life and as my ridiculously over dramatic imagination took over again, I played the whole anaesthetic and operation scenario through in my head with, of course, the worst outcome possible and became fraught at the thought of losing Holly. How on earth would I be able to go on without her? I was thrown into turmoil. What was the right decision for her? Was I handing her a death sentence by agreeing to let the vets operate on her? She was utterly dependent on me to make the right decision for her. It was a dreadful time. However, I had to trust that the vets knew exactly what they were doing and that an operation was in Holly's best interests. After all, she couldn't not have it.

Having worked myself up into such a state, when I dropped her off at the vets in the morning, I promptly burst into tears. Then coming back into the house and she wasn't there, just added to my distress and turmoil. I don't know how I managed to get through the first lesson of that day, but thankfully the vet phoned me as soon as the operation was over. He said Holly was lying at his feet feeling a bit sorry for herself, but everything had gone really well and she was a 'hardy lass'! Thankfully, I got her home around 3pm and never left her side for a good while after that. Mind you, as soon as she got home, she plodded into the kitchen looking for food, so I took that as a good sign. My girl was back.

She recovered incredibly quickly and, I'm happy to say, was back to her cheeky self in no time and milking all the extra care and attention, for what it was worth. Apart from having a bald bottom and looking a bit like a pin cushion from the injections and blood tests, she was soon back to her full glory.

I on the other hand, felt irreversibly traumatised. I know in hindsight, I probably turned a minor problem into a major calamity again, but I had devoted everything to caring for Holly since she came to live with me two years earlier and for people who may not understand the bond and attachment between an owner and their pet, what I went through carried every bit the same emotions and anxieties as a parent watching their child go through an operation. The worry, fear, stress and tears were exactly the same. I told the vet that if and when she ever went in to be spayed, they'd have to give the drugs to me rather than her and have a steady supply of Valium to hand to calm me. I've never been so grateful just to get to the end of a week and still have my beautiful Holly.

HOLLY, THE MAHOGANY GIRL

CHAPTER FIFTEEN
Fairies, Beaches and Wheelchairs

In the spring of 2011, Holly and I had another log cabin break. With the car loaded, Holly, myself and the friend we were travelling with all on board, we headed out of Edinburgh travelling North to our destination. This time, our log cabin was over 1100 feet above sea level and was nestled in a beautiful Glen surrounded by stunning, majestic Scottish mountains at a place called the Spittal of Glenshee in the extreme north east corner of Perthshire. I had been there a few times pre Holly and I knew she would love it. It was one of my favourite places on earth. The area is so remote that if the weather is very bad, the main route there can often be shut off. If that happens, you have to abandon your holiday. Luckily, because it is such a mountainous region, it is a popular ski resort so they try very hard to keep the access road open.

Even if the road is open, it doesn't necessarily mean that it is a straightforward drive. On one of my previous visits, the night before we were due to leave the cabin to head home, there was a very heavy snowfall. Before we could even get on the road, we had to dig the car out. Once on the road, I didn't get out of second gear for a good thirty miles. There was a particularly steep hill to ascend coming out of Glenshee, which often beats the most experienced of drivers, resulting in spinning wheels, rapidly disappearing traction and cars sliding back down the hill. It becomes such a regular occurrence throughout the winter that all the locals come out in force to help push the cars up the hill to keep things moving. It really is a sight to behold and as on that occasion, we were one of the cars that needed a push, we were very grateful for the friendly locals but feared for their backs! Luckily this time, although wintery and snowy, the journey to the log cabin was much more straightforward.

There were four beautiful Norwegian cabins situated in the Glen known more accurately as the Glen of the Fairies. The natural beauty of the area and the spectacular scenery made it an idyllic location. Thankfully we didn't have to endure the frightening weather that we had on the Isle of Seil as this time, throughout our whole stay, the sun shone brightly, splitting clear blue skies above snow capped mountains. Whenever I visited these cabins, I always felt like I'd died and gone to Heaven. Hard to adequately describe the 'feel' of the location; the best words I can use are tranquil, soothing, healing and magical. I loved it.

Glenshee gets its name from the Gaelic word *Shith*, meaning 'fairies'. Up until the late 1800s, the inhabitants were known as *Sithichean A' Ghlinnshith* - 'The Elves of Glenshee'.

There was an ancient meeting place behind the Kirk which was known as the 'Hill of the Fairies' and the 'Fairy Burn' ran down the side of the mountain at the head of Glenshee. In the 1820s, there was a centuries old Chapel at the Spittal of Glenshee called the Chapel of Ease. The church had to be rebuilt and relocated further down the glen. However, every morning the workmen woke to find all their tools scattered and the new foundations destroyed and dispersed. They made several further attempts to continue to relocate the Chapel without success and after much discussion with everyone local to the area, the decision was made to leave the Chapel where it was so as not to antagonise the fairies further and instead they continued to rebuild the new church, but in the same place as it had always been. This course of action proved successful.

This captivating account endured through the years and it is now said that the fairies soon decide whether visitors are welcome or not. Those they choose to accept will become enchanted with the area and continue to return to the Glen for the rest of their lives. Perhaps I met with the fairies approval as I love the Glen so much I would live there if I could and if they would let me!

There is a lovely line on the History section of the Glen of the Fairies website that says 'the visitor must beware….if the fairies like you, and cast their spell, then you will be forced to always return to our enchanted glen....' This may explain why it felt like such an entrancing and magical location.

We unloaded the car and settled into the cabin. Holly made herself comfortable very quickly and familiarised herself to her new surroundings – well the main crucial areas of importance to her – the couch and the fridge, while my friend and I planned the next few days.

We were spoilt for choice. The wonderful location gave us access to Blairgowrie and Braemar as well as Royal Deeside – Crathie Church, the Royal family's favourite place of worship when in the area and of course the Queen's special retreat, Balmoral Castle. Perhaps we could join Ma'am for afternoon tea and Holly could meet the Corgis. On second thoughts, maybe not – Her Majesty would be none too amused if Holly swiped the Royal Shortbread off the tea tray before it was served. I bet the Corgis never behaved like that, perhaps they could teach Holly some Royal Canine Etiquette.

There were also the beautiful Perthshire towns of Pitlochry and Dunkeld, Dunkeld being the ancient capital of Scotland. Then of course there were all the castles Blair, Glamis and Scone Palace – Blair Castle having its own private army, the Atholl Highlanders who held regular parades. We would never fit everything in during our short stay.

We decided not to spoil our trip by cramming too much in but had lovely leisurely drives enjoying the incredible scenery and local landmarks.

All three of us began to unwind and relax in the beautiful location. However, I had a niggling worry in my mind that just wouldn't go away. One morning, I had taken Holly out for a little stroll so she could stretch her legs and attend to business matters. As we walked up the path round the back of the cabin, which was on a very slight incline, she gave a little whimper. The previous afternoon, when we'd been sitting outside a little café enjoying a coffee, Holly had sat down at my feet and made a similar noise. Apart from these two little incidents, everything else seemed fine. She seemed happy and cheerful and was enjoying double helpings of morning cuddles as my friend loved dogs as much as I did. Holly lapped up the extra attention and very quickly had two servants under her command for the holiday.

However, I knew my dog so well, even if she tried to ignore that something wasn't right, I couldn't. Whatever was going on seemed to be a minor annoyance to Holly but of course, the worry wagon was making its way through my head again and picking up speed. Soon it would be thundering through like a freight train.

Given Holly's history and special needs, whenever we went away anywhere, I would always make sure I knew where the nearest vet was and had all their contact details to hand. I would let my vet know, just in case the worst happened and they had to provide Holly's medical history to another vet. I would make sure I knew the location of the nearest payphone should I not be able to get a mobile phone signal or internet access. I didn't think the situation was that serious on this occasion and we'd be home in a couple of days anyway. However, to put my mind at rest, I phoned my vet to make an appointment for the day we got home. Sometimes I wish that was a call I'd never made and Holly and I could have just frozen time there and then and stayed forever in the magical, trouble and stress free Glen of the Fairies, together forever more.

The rest of our break passed with no further issues and we had an uneventful journey back home. The next day, I took Holly straight to the vets.

As usual, Holly was delighted to see everyone and they her. The staff who had known her from the very first visit when she lumbered and waddled into their reception marvelled at her continuing transformation and I beamed with pride. After receiving due adoration from her fans, Holly's vet called her into his consulting room. After the pair greeted each other enthusiastically and the vet also commented on how good she was looking, I explained what had happened while we were away. My vet was always extremely thorough and ensured he covered all bases. Holly truly got five star treatment and she deserved it. The vet suggested I book her in to have a small sedative so he could give her a couple of x-rays and run a few tests. This was arranged and we just had to wait a few days for the results.

My cousin, her daughter and I had agreed to visit Yellowcraigs beach later that week, after the visit to the vets. Holly and I absolutely loved Yellowcraigs. It was one of if not the most beautiful beach in East Lothian and could be accessed from a lovely forested area near North Berwick. To get to the beach, you walked along the forest paths then over a grassy area up to the sand dunes before scrambling down to the beach. It was very popular with dog walkers, locals and tourists alike. In a way, it was something else that had become symbolic of Holly's progress over the years. I had taken her down there in the early days on one of the longer walks we tried to tackle, when she was still topping the scales at ten stone. Poor Holly didn't even make it through the forest. She could walk a few steps then had to lie down she was so exhausted. She would lie panting heavily until she regained a bit more energy to get to her feet again and to walk a few more steps. It was heart-breaking to see her so debilitated. Clearly at that time the 'long-ish' walk I had in mind for her was out of the question, I was so worried that I'd just about killed her. We had no choice but to start heading back to the car having covered a fraction of the walk I'd hoped we'd do. I prayed she'd make it back to the car. I made a little note in my mind to look into buying a platform trolley for Holly to sit on, just in case we found ourselves in this position again.

This visit, however, was a completely different story. As soon as we all arrived at the car park and I opened the door, Holly shot out of the car and started running off towards the forest.

It was us running to catch up with her this time rather than her struggling through every tortured step. It was so wonderful to see and again I felt so proud of my dog, her fighting spirit and her new found love of life.

Holly liked to thoroughly examine every blade of grass and give each tree her undivided attention for a good five minutes, so after her initial sprint to the forest, the pace slowed a little as we all enjoyed the beautiful surroundings. Once we reached the sand dunes and Holly saw the beach and the sea, again, there was no stopping her. I could tell she was torn – should she run straight to the water, or go and introduce herself to some of the other dogs there first. While she decided, she barked to let everyone know she'd arrived and then started running. I just loved watching her run. Considering she'd barely been able to walk, it was a great sight. It was rather comical too though I must say. She did try very hard to keep up with all the other dogs, but never quite managed. She would do her funny, lopsided gallop over to what or whoever happened to catch her attention then almost grind to a halt, as if she'd surprised herself with her own mobility. I never saw her swim but she did love to paddle. With her new found bravado and attitude she would wade in so far, if she was brave, until the water was up to her belly, but as soon as there was a hint of water being splashed on her face she would come back out again, looking rather disgruntled. She was such a funny mixture. She could put on such a tough, blasé exterior when meeting new dogs or facing new situations, but the minute something unnerved her or took her by surprise, she would come back to me for reassurance.

Holly and my cousin's daughter had great fun paddling together and playing with sticks. It was like they had each found a new best friend. It was a wonderful day, another really happy memory.

Right up until my mobile rang. It was the vet. Holly's results were back.

As I took the call and watched Holly and my little cousin frolicking around in the sea, I couldn't take in or comprehend what the vet was telling me. Holly's x-rays had shown that she had severe hip dysplasia, arthritis and spondylosis of the spine a condition where bone spurs, which are bony projections, can form along joints in the spine and if it is quite widespread, the vertebrae can weld into a rigid, inflexible backbone. I will never forget the vets next words 'Holly's case is quite severe – if she were a human, she'd be in a wheelchair.' What? Say that again? I couldn't believe it. As I watched Holly try to catch a stick as it splashed and bobbed about in the waves, I said to the vet 'you must have the wrong dog, the x-rays must have got mixed up.' As if all that wasn't enough to take in, while she'd been in, they'd scanned her liver as they'd felt it was a little enlarged and taken some bloods.

The results of Holly's liver blood tests would always confuse me greatly as they were so complex, but I understood the enormity of part of what the vet was telling me during that call. Her ALT's, the enzyme that indicates liver damage should never be more than around sixty and Holly's reading had come back at nine hundred and thirty! She was off the scale.

I think I was in shock. There had been no indications whatsoever of anything of this nature in the blood tests she had at the very beginning that showed up her hypothyroidism. Surely her liver should have been even healthier now that she had lost all that weight and was much fitter. What on earth had I done wrong?

As soon as I could, I was to go down and pick up some medications to see if we could treat whatever was going on with Holly's liver. As I stood rooted to the spot having hung up the phone, I realised I had a very soggy doggy standing at my feet, tongue hanging out, grinning wildly and wagging her tail furiously waiting for me to play with her. How could the diagnosis I'd just been given fit the lively, boisterous dog that was at my feet? Hadn't we already had a big enough uphill battle? Hadn't she been through enough? When was my poor dog going to get a break? If I was heartened by anything that day, it was that Holly was no ordinary dog, nothing would beat her. She had a fight and a determination in her that I'd rarely come across before in humans or animals. She and I were a strong team.

We'd come through a lot together already and we'd get out the other end of this latest crisis too.

CHAPTER SIXTEEN
Doggy Fry Ups

In my more troubled moments, I would beat myself up thinking I must be the worst dog owner in the world. I had taken on a dog whose main problem was that she was grossly obese and I'd made her more ill. In my more rational moments, I knew that was silly, I had no way of knowing what would lie ahead for Holly and had I not taken her into my care in the summer of 2008, I doubt she would have lived much longer. It was just all so hard at times. I felt from day one, we were putting out fires with her health. She'd get over one ailment, then develop another. As a side effect of her thyroid problems, she had also started to develop muscular atrophy which caused gradual wastage of her skull resulting in eye problems that needed attention. She had constant issues with her ears meaning regular cleaning and drops. And now this latest blow of joint and skeletal problems and the major worry of what was going on with her liver. I think she was going for the record for the dog with the most health problems in the world. At one point after the vets latest diagnosis, she developed a short bout of giardia, an easily treated intestinal infection, very common in dogs and for that matter, humans too, but on top of everything else Holly and I were battling against, it almost felt like the last straw. Once we had picked up Holly's latest batch of medicines, my house was rapidly beginning to resemble a veterinary surgery. I was feeling like a full-time veterinary nurse and at the peak of Holly's treatment requirements, I was administering twenty-seven pills a day, ear drops and eye drops and providing her with physio twice a day. I had to put a list up on the kitchen wall, detailing her full medicinal regimen to ensure I did everything right and didn't forget anything. I was convinced I was going to put something in her mouth that should be in her ear and something up her nose that should go in her eye. However, we stayed the steadfast team we had always been and we managed. I think Holly must have somehow known and begun to understand that all this made her feel better and I was always in awe of the fact that she would sit peacefully and quietly while I administered her treatment.

Considering more often than not, she was now full of beans, loved playing and rarely did as she was told, yet whenever I walked from the kitchen through to the living room and said to her, 'Holly come through and get your ear and eye drops in,' like the most obedient dog in the world, she would follow me through and sit good as gold at my feet, patiently waiting for her medicine to be administered. This never failed to amaze me as on nearly every other occasion when I asked her to do something she would completely ignore me. As I moved in to put her eardrops in, I would always get the 'paw of pity' when she would lift her little paw up, whether for reassurance or in the vain hope that she could temporarily distract me from what I was doing by looking suitably cute and pathetic, I don't know, but it would always break my heart. If she was able to rest her paw on my forearm as I administered her drops, it seemed to pacify her a little. It was almost as if she wanted to help me put the drops in, like a child holding the spoon in her mother's hand as they both, together put the medicine into the child's mouth.

Although one of the medicines Holly had been prescribed was Hepatosyl, a liver support supplement, the vet had told me that cottage cheese would also be good for her liver and I could start to introduce this into her diet. So, much to her delight, Holly was then regularly treated to cottage cheese. I would have done anything, anything to help keep my best friend well.

The vet was always very honest with me, he never sugar coated anything but he was always, always positive. He never gave up on Holly and without fail, went the extra mile, when I feel others may have given up. He too was alarmed at the level of Holly's ALT results and was concerned that her liver may just crash and if that happened, it may be too late to help her. He told me what warning signs to look out for that would indicate that her liver was really struggling – vomiting, diarrhoea, yellow eyes, gums, ears and skin, lethargy and loss of appetite. Holly showed none of these symptoms, in fact, quite the opposite – she looked the picture of health.

We were left with a real dilemma. Steroids may help Holly's joints but they would damage her liver further. A liver biopsy was suggested but this filled me with horror. Apart from her little bottom operation, I had kept my girl safe and well enough that she hadn't had to go through major surgery. When discussing this option, I'd asked if an ultrasound guided needle biopsy would be an alternative less traumatic option, but was told it would in fact be a higher risk procedure for Holly as we may not get an accurate result and there was the risk of nicking another organ.

The vet advised me that if we were going to do the biopsy it had to be a full laparotomy and we should do it sooner rather than later. The procedure would involve a large incision through the abdominal wall to gain access to her liver through her abdominal cavity.

My heart sank. I wanted the ground to swallow me up. Agreeing to her having her little bottom abscess dealt with was hard enough, this was utter torture.

I was advised that there was a chance I would be potentially shortening her life by not agreeing to the biopsy. However, I was also told that there was the possibility that the biopsy could prove inconclusive and her treatment would stay exactly the same. In other words, she would be put through major surgery for nothing.

The small glimmers of hope were that Holly's liver would still be able to function even with a lot of problems and like a human liver, it could regenerate and heal itself in time.

I thought long and hard and after a number of sleepless nights, I decided I couldn't agree to the biopsy. If it would have produced guaranteed answers as to what was wrong with Holly and a proven cure, then the decision would have been a lot easier. But while there was the distinct possibility she would go through it all for nothing to change, I just couldn't do that to her. None of this would have come to light had I not decided to have the cause of her little whimpers at the log cabin checked out – we would have been none the wiser and carried on as normal, oblivious to all these problems.

Outwardly, Holly was still thriving, looking glorious and appearing happier and healthier than ever. You would never know to look at her about what felt like the bomb that had just gone off inside her.

The vet was so patient with me as I reached my decision. He knew exactly what Holly meant to me and how much we'd been through together. Between us we agreed to keep things as they were, maintain Holly's current treatment plan and monitor her closely.

It helped to have made the decision and decide on a way forward, so Holly was booked in for regular liver blood tests from that point on. As we waited for her results to come back each time, the vet and I held our breath. I think we were both mightily relieved when Holly's ALT reading slowly but surely began to come down.

Again, I felt so bad that Holly had to go through blood tests every three to six months but any and every decision I made for her was with her best interests at heart and given the seriousness of her latest condition, she really had to be closely monitored.

To enable them to carry out these particular blood tests, Holly's blood was tested first thing in the morning to get a base line. She was then given a very high fat meal and her blood tested again a couple of hours later so they could tell how well her liver worked at breaking down the fat.

Before each trip I would try to make it more fun for Holly by telling her she'd be getting her 'doggy fry up' or her 'full English breakfast.' I hoped, given her boring diet of late, this may cheer her up a little, and make the visits to the vets a bit more enjoyable – that and the attention she would have showered on her by her Private Health Care Team.

As her liver results fell, although they were still far too high, they were more stable so I asked if the bloods could be done less regularly. I just didn't want Holly to go through more than she absolutely had to. We would continue treating her as we were as it was obviously working.

The most important thing was that I wanted whatever time Holly had left to be quality time and despite everything, despite her constant health battles, she had become one of the happiest and friendliest dogs I'd ever known. I owed it to her to give her as good a life as I possibly could.

HOLLY, THE MAHOGANY GIRL

CHAPTER SEVENTEEN
Pet Therapy

Holly's and my lives continued as they always had. We were two halves of a whole. We both adapted to her new medicinal routine without any major mishaps and thankfully nothing ended up where it shouldn't have been. Every pill and drop reached its correct destination. Holly still loved her walks and continued to work her magic on the neighbours, playing them beautifully for biscuits. One of Holly's favourite neighbours had actually begun to join us on walks and we enjoyed the company – Holly especially, as it meant extra treats for her.

I couldn't help but laugh when Holly developed a new routine as she started getting used to her new friend joining us on walks. As we reached the lady's house, Holly would stand in the middle of their lawn, bolt upright, staring straight into their living room window until the lady noticed and came out. If she didn't come out quickly enough, Holly would start barking. Once anyone was part of 'Team Holly' – they had to dance to her tune.

It was just as well the lady loved it and couldn't wait for Holly's visits or I would have been mortified. It was difficult to explain to Holly what was happening if the lady happened to be out when we went our walks, and those particular strolls took a lot longer as Holly would stop every few steps and turn around to see if the lady might be behind us trying to catch up with us. Worst case scenario, Holly would just sit down and refuse to move – willing the lady (and her biscuits) to come running round the corner. A quick walk, could take a long time on those days!

Holly hoping her favourite neighbour (and her biscuits) may appear round the corner

Since that fateful day on Yellowcraigs beach, the worry over Holly's liver condition which had technically meant that Holly was now in chronic liver failure, had dominated my thoughts. I hadn't given too much thought to her skeletal problems as they really didn't seem to be bothering her much and she had been put on Tramadol to manage any pain or discomfort she may have been feeling. Although vastly smaller than she had been, Holly was still a big dog and her back legs in particular had always looked a bit bowed under the weight, but her sessions on the underwater treadmill had really strengthened her joints and she had good muscle definition. When she walked, she had an extremely impressive swagger and I always felt she could fairly swing a kilt if given half the chance.

If I had noticed anything, it may have been that she was slowing a little on her walks and maybe she was a little stiffer, so we simply adjusted speed and duration as and when required – after all, neither of us were getting any younger. However, she was still highly spirited and enthusiastic, especially when other dogs walked past and clearly always saw herself as the boss of the neighbourhood.

I felt our most recent frightening crisis had passed, for the moment anyway, and I wanted to focus on continuing to give Holly a happy and comfortable life.

I had bought a little set of caravan steps to help her when she needed to get in and out of the car or wanted to get on the couch. She used these perfectly and with ease for the car, but as usual, had her own ideas when it came to getting on her beloved couch. She had perfected her technique of getting her front paws on the seat then shuffling forward on her back paws to get closer, then standing on her tip toes to raise one leg up onto the seat, balancing, then pulling the other one up to then make herself comfortable in her favourite place. She had it down to a fine art and wasn't about to use a daft set of steps!

In the cold winter evenings and mornings, the decking at my back door leading out into the garden could become very slippery. To make sure Holly didn't lose her grip and fall, I put an old carpet down for her to walk on, but Holly, being Holly, just walked round it. Holly was her own boss, she had her own ways and methods of doing things and she was going to stick to them. There is no doubt that it was this unbending spirit and determination that made her such a fighter.

Holly's strength of spirit and resilience had begun to rub off on me too. She taught me so much but most of all, once you set your mind to something, don't let anything get in your way until you achieve your goal and never, ever give up, even if all the odds are stacked against you.

The positive impact we had on each other saw us both evolve over the years. Holly's arrival in my life provided stability, routine and purpose again after so many difficult years. Watching her embrace her second chance at life inspired me to do the same and in 2011 –

I at last fulfilled my long held ambition to set up my own charity for bears which went from strength to strength and continues to do so.

Both our lives were unrecognisable from the lives we'd been living when we came together in 2008. I had always had great respect for the work of Therapy Pets and Assistance Animals and the devotion of these pets to their owners. Holly had most definitely been my therapy pet and much, much more.

As we both grew a little older we would, together, face whatever the next few years would bring and I pledged to ensure she would have whatever care she needed to continue to give her the highest quality of life that she so deserved.

We had shared so much together and were about to have another enthralling shared experience.

HOLLY, THE MAHOGANY GIRL

CHAPTER EIGHTEEN
Hot Stuff!

Her Ladyship and I were about to enjoy a little light entertainment. For longer than I can remember, I'd been meaning to get one of these fire safety checks done that you see advertised on the television. I think I tend to lean towards the obsessive compulsive when it comes to making sure everything is switched off before I go out or before bedtime.

I had become particularly prone to this behaviour ever since Holly had graced the house with her presence. I always worried constantly about things that could happen to her. I would never leave her alone in the car, or tied up outside a shop and the risk of fire when I was out leaving her stuck inside the house, was most definitely one of my greatest concerns.

I was chatting about organising a safety check with one of my pupils, whose father just happened to be a local fireman, 'Oh don't worry', she exclaimed, 'My dad will do that for you.' Wonderful, I thought, that's that sorted.

Having always had a fondness for men in uniform and in particular, knights in shining armour who wouldn't think twice about rescuing you from a burning building, I jokingly said, 'Do you think he'll bring the fire engine?' followed by, 'Do you think he could bring the whole crew?' before I pulled myself together and gave myself a gentle reminder that this was a serious matter. The arrangements were made and a date was set for 7pm the following Wednesday.

After a week of furious housework, Wednesday 7pm came and went and no ring of the doorbell. As I sat mildly disappointed, it dawned on me that they must have had a call out, after all, they did have a few things more important to do than check my windows and doors. Not to worry, I could always rearrange.

Imagine my delight, when a couple of minutes later, a big, shiny red fire engine drew up outside my door and as if that wasn't excitement enough, three strapping firemen, all kitted up, piled out of the magnificent machine. 'Nothing like a fire engine and a few firemen to brighten up a lady's evening,' I said to Holly as she sat on the couch beside me, listening intently as if she understood the significance of the moment. Goodness knows what the neighbours were thinking.

As I was chatting to the fireman, who was the father of my pupil, and trying very hard to maintain an air of professionalism whilst surrounded by firemen and as I thought I was going to faint, we discussed escape routes should the worst happen.

I expressed my concerns to him about what would happen if there was a fire when I was out and Holly was trapped in the house. I said, 'I know I don't have any right to ask you to risk your life to save my dog, but would you?!'. 'Oh don't worry', he replied, 'We rescue dogs all the time', heart pounding and verging on a swooning state, the words 'my hero' floated around in my head, 'Mind you', he continued, 'I might need to get one of the lads to give her a Fireman's lift, she's a big girl!'

I was now officially jealous of my dog.

They did a tremendous job, giving me lots of valuable advice and fitting two new smoke detectors with ten-year batteries, all free of charge. It was an extremely worthwhile exercise.

As these knights in shining armour left my living room, I followed them out with Holly to go for our evening walk. I had to give myself a swift kick to stop myself from asking if I could have a shot in the fire engine.

It's funny how you never really grow up when it comes to situations like these.

So, as we nonchalantly waived them off, thinking, this'll get the neighbours talking, Holly and I enjoyed our evening stroll, knowing we would sleep a bit more soundly that night, safe in the knowledge that we had a wonderful local fire department.

HOLLY, THE MAHOGANY GIRL

CHAPTER NINETEEN
Swinging Kilts

My work load was beginning to increase as my business picked up. To try and compensate for the cancellations that inevitably always came, I usually booked in more lessons than I would normally like to do, working on the basis that some of them may cancel. If for any reason, there was a day I couldn't get home, I had found Holly the most wonderful 'Doggy Nanny'. Because Holly's needs were so specific and because she couldn't walk as far or fast as other dogs, none of the 'standard' dog walking services would take her. Their normal practices seemed to be to take big groups of dogs for long beach walks that lasted over an hour. I knew Holly would never be able to cope with this and it would do her more harm than good. I couldn't bear the thought of her trying to keep up with all the other dogs and hurting herself in the process.

So we found a wonderful lady who provided a second to none service. She was perfect for Holly. She would take Holly out on her own on Holly's little familiar walks in her own neighbourhood. She would also give her her medicine and lunch if needed and although Holly and I had never had a day or night apart in all our time together, I always worried about what I would do if I had to go away overnight for whatever reason, or God forbid, I had to go into hospital. Once I found Holly's 'Doggy Nanny', those problems were solved too. If needed she would come and stay in the house overnight with Holly, so Holly would be able to stay in her own familiar surroundings. She also drove an 'Animal Ambulance' so should the worst happen when Holly was in her care, she would be able to get her to the vet immediately. This greatly put my mind at rest as although I had no plans to go away, I knew this may happen in the future and I hoped I would have Holly for a good few years yet, so I just wanted to try and plan ahead for all eventualities. There is no way I would have put Holly in kennels, apart from anything else, she would take one look and wonder where her reclining sofa was.

Holly loved her new nanny and although we didn't need to call on her often, it was a relief to know that she was there if we needed her.

Holly did seem to manage to cast a spell on everyone she met. One of my lovely pupils had forgotten to pay me at the end of her lesson. She and her fiancé had just booked their wedding for July 2014 and we'd excitedly been chatting about it and completely forgot to settle up for the lesson. She rang me as soon as she realised. She noticed before I did as I was heading straight home to get Holly as she was due down at the vets for one of her check-ups.

As my pupil's house was on the way to the vets, I said I would pop in en route to pick up payment. Holly was in the back of the car and in her usual excited, exuberant way, barked her greeting when she met my pupil and lapped up the ensuing cuddles.

The next time I picked my pupil up for a lesson she got in the car and said, 'I have something to ask you, well Holly really… we've been discussing arrangements for the wedding and we would love it if Holly would be our ring bearer.' I almost squealed with delight. I could just imagine how much Holly would adore being the centre of attention and could picture her walking up the aisle with her little ring pouch. Perhaps she'd get to swing that kilt after all! 'She'd love to,' I replied, once again, feeling very proud of my girl being chosen to be such an important part of someone's big day.

HOLLY, THE MAHOGANY GIRL

CHAPTER TWENTY
The Unfinished Walk

Towards the end of May 2012, despite all our efforts to keep her problems at bay, Holly's multitude of health issues began to catch up with her. We set off on our evening walk on a lovely warm night. The weather had been really gorgeous of late and we would wait until a little later in the evening, when it had cooled down a bit, for Holly's bedtime stroll. I put her collar and lead on, grabbed some poop bags and we shut the door behind us. It really was a beautiful night – a far cry from the many, many winter walks we'd had to endure together in the cold biting wind and snow.

Feeling relaxed and happy with my companion, we headed up the road on her familiar walk. As was the norm, Holly stopped to thoroughly sniff and examine every tree, bush and blade of grass en route in case there had been any significant changes since she last checked them out.

I felt she was walking a little slower than normal, but

I put that down to the unusually warm weather.

We continued round the corner to head down to her favourite grassy bit on the main road. As we turned the corner, Holly walked a few more steps and then just sat down for no apparent reason. This was really quite unusual and hadn't happened during walks since the early days. I went back to give her a cuddle and said, 'Are you okay girl, what's the matter?'. Something wasn't right. Perhaps it was still too warm for her. She'd been lying out in the garden most of the day, maybe she'd got a little sunstroke. Holly definitely wasn't herself. Despite having to deal with Holly's many ailments and treatments, I knew what was her 'normal' level of health and what was her standard response to not feeling quite right and we always managed. But this was different. She looked tired and beaten. I couldn't get her to budge. I couldn't get her to stand, never mind walk – even after giving her time to rest. I began to feel the panic setting in. The vets words echoed in my head, 'if she were a human, she'd be in a wheelchair' – still so hard to take in, especially as when I first heard them, I was with Holly and she was running around on the beach and this quick deterioration had come on so suddenly.

What was I going to do? I had to get her back to the house, then I could call the vet out, but she couldn't walk. Should I tie her lead to a lamppost and run home to get the car? If I did that, how on earth would I get her in the car and the last thing I wanted to do was leave her on her own. I had no choice but to run to a neighbour for help.

This I did, and between us, we managed to entice Holly to her feet and gently and gingerly get her back round the corner and on to the final short stretch back to the house. She had to sit down at regular intervals but we made slow and steady progress. By this time a number of the other neighbours had seen poor Holly struggling and they came running out to help too. So many people cared about her and I found it so touching. Having watched her transform over the years from an ill dog to a healthy dog, it looked like they were beginning to witness her gradual decline again.

All I could focus on was getting her home and slowly but surely we managed. One of my neighbours waited with me until the vet came out. Sadly, because it was an out of hours emergency call out, it was a vet we didn't know. I had been advised that I could increase Holly's Tramadol if I felt it was needed and on this occasion, it certainly was. I didn't like to if I didn't have to, as I knew she could sometimes react badly to it – almost like she was having a bad 'trip' and this was hard to watch too.

I explained Holly's complex history to the vet and he thoroughly examined her to make sure nothing was broken. He felt because, as so often happens in Scotland with little warning, the weather had gone from very cold to very warm in a matter of days, and like anyone troubled with arthritis and joint problems, this was simply a flare up for Holly.

I'm not sure if it was because we'd managed to get back to the house which made me a little calmer and so, as a result, Holly seemed a little calmer, or if it was the additional Tramadol kicking in, but she seemed to be a bit more settled and more at ease as the vet checked her over. Just to be on the safe side, he gave her an injection of Metacam to alleviate her joint inflammation and pain.

He obviously noticed Holly's bedding on the couch. I explained to him that her decision to sleep there was of her own accord, even if I made a bed up for her on the floor, she would always opt for the couch. I made it clear that I never forced her or made her feel that she had to get up on the couch to please me, the choice was all hers, indeed, heaven help anyone who tried to stop her.

He was clearly very troubled by Holly's condition, probably compounded by not knowing her and this being their first meeting. He said to me, 'I think you should probably accept the fact that she'll never get up on the couch again.' I was equally as worried and alarmed by the evening's events and nodded my acknowledgement of the seriousness of the situation.

Five minutes after the vet left, Holly was back on the couch. Like I said, she had her own way of doing things.

To my immense relief, Holly slept extremely soundly, I think she was probably stoned on painkillers, but they certainly helped and in the morning she seemed a lot brighter. As soon as the surgery was open, I phoned Holly's regular vet and talked everything through with him. He prescribed complete rest for Holly for a good while and to keep up her pain medication while we got through this bad spell.

Although better than she was, Holly was extremely subdued. Luckily for the most part, the weather for the next few weeks was lovely, so she just lay quietly in the sun out in the garden. For a dog that was normally pretty vocal, which on occasion could test my patience, the sudden silence was deafening.

Lying outside, she was content and comfortable but so quiet and all of a sudden, the impact of the events of the last few days hit me and the deathly quiet made me realise what it would feel like when she wasn't here. It was the first time I had seriously had to face the prospect as up until then, I'd focused one hundred percent on getting her fit and well in preparation for a long happy life.

Given her latest diagnosis and prognosis, the enormity of what had just happened and the clear indication that things were beginning to deteriorate, the thought of losing her hit me hard. As I stood in the kitchen, looking at her resting peacefully in the garden in the shade of her favourite bush, I was overwhelmed by sadness. I stumbled through to the living room so she wouldn't see me or hear me and burst into tears. It was a real physical ache in the pit of my stomach.

I had fought so hard for her, for her future and for our future together. It seemed like she'd been with me for such a short time and it felt like I was already beginning to lose her.

Holly resting in her favourite spot in the garden

Holly being Holly, of course, had different ideas. It took time but after lots of love, care and attention and weeks of rest, she began to rally. Her energy and sparkle returned and soon, when I got up in the mornings, once again, she would be standing waiting for me in the middle of the living room floor for 'morning cuddles', tail wagging furiously. Holly was making a comeback.

Six weeks to the day, we managed to finish the walk we'd started at the end of May. It was such a momentous occasion that this time, my mum who was visiting for the day and a couple of the neighbours joined us! Holly was almost beside herself with excitement. I was trying hard to be the responsible parent and tell her to take it easy and I asked our fellow walkers to keep things at a slow pace so Holly didn't overdo it.

Who was I kidding? The minute we were out the front door – off she shot at the full length of her extending lead and it was us having trouble keeping up with her!

Holly setting the pace!

HOLLY, THE MAHOGANY GIRL

CHAPTER TWENTY ONE
The Comeback Queen

Over the next few months Holly made remarkable progress. On the vets instructions we did little walks as and when Holly could manage them. Some days, Holly had more energy than others so between us, we formulated a plan. We had three 'Holly sized walks' depending on what she could do on any given day.

The first one was literally just a few yards from the house. It was a little grassy area where she could relieve herself if she didn't want to go too far. The second was her walk round the small block and the third was an extended version of that walk which went a little further down the road to another grassy area and back again.

If we had to decide between walk number two or three we would need to make that decision at the corner of our road and very often, on her good days, Holly made her decision to go on walk number three before I did as she very subtly, some distance before the corner, started to make her way across the road to ensure I understood exactly what she wanted.

On some occasions, if I was in a hurry and really only had time to do the middle-sized walk, a battle of wills would ensue between us on that corner. Needless to say, she usually won but it was hard not to give in to her, I was just pleased she felt well enough to do the longer walk. One day as she was starting to cross the road to tell me she wanted to do the longer walk, we became aware of a young family coming out of a house over the road, they had obviously been visiting friends and were getting the children back into the car. Holly became aware of the man coming over to say hello to her and again, she was beside herself with excitement. You can just tell when people love dogs and it filled Holly with glee whenever anyone came to speak to her. She would start spinning around like a helicopter blade and loved the extra cuddles – a far cry from the sad, withdrawn dog I met all those years ago that would shy away from affection.

I was aware the man was on crutches as he hopped over to see us. I wasn't really taking the whole situation in and thought he must have a broken leg but other than that, nothing registered, I was just so over the moon at Holly's high spirits and return to good health.

Of course, Holly did her usual, and with great enthusiasm, starting going through the man's legs to get a bottom rub. I feared she would knock the man off his crutches as he started to wobble, trying to maintain his balance but loving Holly's special game. As was always necessary in these embarrassing situations, I had to rapidly explain what Holly was doing – that it was one of her favourite tricks to go through people's legs. It was then reality dawned – the reason the man was on crutches was that he only had one leg! Oh I wanted the ground to swallow me up. What on earth should I say now? However, everyone was roaring and laughing at Holly and the man seemed completely unaffected, so I thought, best say nothing more and move swiftly on as we waved everyone goodbye!! It was one of the many comical situations I found myself in with Holly and I'm so grateful the man saw the funny side too and made things easier for me to save my embarrassment. Holly, on the other hand was completely oblivious of her faux pas! We were just both extremely relieved the gentleman had remained upright.

At the other end of the scale of Holly's walk lengths, if she wasn't having such a good day she would tell me quite clearly that she only wanted to go to the grassy bit beside our house and when she was done, she would start walking home again to take up residence on the sofa for the rest of the day.

She really never failed to amaze me. She knew precisely what I'd been trying to do for her by devising the walks of different lengths and she found a way to tell me exactly what she wanted and needed to do.

Since her bad spell at the end of May, the vet had been trying very hard to decide on what course to take next with Holly's treatment. The Metacam had seemed to work wonders but there was a real risk to her liver if she was put on it long term. I popped into the surgery to have a chat with him. He suggested a course of Cartrophen injections which were used to treat arthritic and geriatric dogs suffering from joint pain, osteoarthritis, hip dysplasia and general joint deterioration. It was a non-steroidal drug which meant it could be used despite Holly's liver problems. It was a course of four injections given over four weeks and could be repeated every three months. I'd also bought Holly a massive tub of Glycoflex tablets which I ground up for her every morning with a pestle and mortar and put in some soft cheese wrapped in ham. This was supposed to work wonders too for dogs with joint problems so we hoped both these treatments would help and she was booked in for her first injection.

The sight of Holly, struggling so much that May evening, haunted me. I asked the vet the question I didn't want to ask because I dreaded the answer. People always say that because we can put animals out of their misery when they are ill and suffering, what a blessing this is. However, at that time, I could only see it as a curse. How on earth was I ever going to be able to know when the time was right, especially when, given a few weeks to recover, Holly always managed to bounce back?

Despite everything, Holly was incredibly happy and always fought so hard to get better and still got so much enjoyment from life. However, I couldn't ignore the hard facts. I almost couldn't believe it myself – the amount of health problems Holly had and the number of treatments she had to go through and the medication she had to have on a daily basis just to keep everything under control, the last thing I wanted her to do was suffer. I never wanted to prolong her suffering to delay my own and I felt, as a responsible dog owner, it was a question I couldn't avoid asking. I was just dreading it, as I didn't want to hear what the vet may tell me. I looked him in the eye and said, 'You will guide me won't you and tell me when you think she's had enough?' My relief at his reply was palpable, 'Oh no, we're not there yet, we've still got these new treatments to try and we'd be doing her a great disservice if we gave up on her.'

Compared to what I was dreading I'd hear, I couldn't have wished for a better answer at that time.

Holly continued to do well with the Cartrophen injections and life went on. We continued to have walks that she loved over distances she could comfortably cover. She was allowed plenty rest and got an abundance of cuddles.

Around September or October of 2012 she went a bit downhill again, around three months after the injections for her joints had been started so their effect must have been wearing off a little. This spell was probably on a par with the one in May, but I was more emotionally and mentally able to cope with it. I knew what to do this time – continue her medication and up her painkillers if needed. I gave her the physio exercises the vet had suggested and allowed her plenty peace and quiet. I knew from previous episodes, that eventually it would pass. As with humans, weather changes can take a toll on those suffering from arthritis and summer was moving into autumn, bringing slightly cooler weather.

True to form, after plenty rest, care, attention and the odd back massage, Holly began to recover. On some mornings I gave her 'breakfast in bed' – when she wouldn't get off the couch to eat her breakfast, I would hold her food in my cupped hands and bring it to her mouth for her to eat what she could manage.

No doubt the dog behaviourists would be cringing again, but I didn't care. I wanted to make sure my dog ate and kept her strength up. Holly made another comeback and soon we were back to our walks, once more, tailored to what she could manage. I made a mental note that if this was going to happen every three months or so, we would probably be due another bad bout at Christmas. I would be taking time off then, so if she did indeed have another bad spell, I would be around to care for her every day. I just prayed it wouldn't happen.

CHAPTER TWENTY TWO
Christmas 2012

October and November came and went with relative ease. The seasons changed, the nights drew in and the temperatures began to drop. Winter was upon us again and most of our walks became relatively short as it was so cold and both of us just wanted to be back home in the warm house. Holly had a lot less padding to keep her warm than she had once had, I, on the other hand, seemed to expand and contract with the weather. My dog had always outshone me when it had come to dieting.

December arrived and I began to look forward to some time off work. I always liked to take a few weeks off at Christmas. It was my favourite time of the year and Holly and I would always have great fun with present wrapping and unwrapping – I would wrap then she would promptly unwrap.

It was a good time to take a break as inevitably bookings would slow down as people began to feel the financial pressures of that time of year. Teaching could also be heavy going weather wise, especially with snow and ice. So I decided to take a three-week break this time. Given the difficult year Holly and I had just had, I wanted us to have some good quality time together. I hoped more than anything that she would stay well and we could enjoy some lovely daytime walks if we got the magical crisp sunny days that we loved so much during the winter months.

December 21st, arrived and with it my last lessons for 2012. With a sigh of relief, I finished teaching for the year. I'd had a really rotten Christmas break the year before and was ill for most of it. Soon after I finished work for my 2011 seasonal break, I happened to lift something the wrong way and my back went out. It was an old injury, sustained from my days with my personal trainer. I was stupidly trying to prove a point while I was working on the leg press – I wanted to prove I could lift all the weight blocks on the machine. It was a ridiculous weight, something like 200kg – 18 or 19 stone. It was extremely stupid of me but when I get an idea in my head, I can be quite stubborn. Well I suffered greatly for my foolhardiness and, as a result, damaged the sacroiliac joint in my lower back. I had to wait months and months for a physio appointment (I should have just booked in at the vets!) and was eventually given exercises to strengthen my back but was warned to be careful in the future.

So, shortly after starting my Christmas break in 2011, I hurt my back again and it was excruciating. On top of this, I had a flare up of raging toothache so was thoroughly miserable. Holly was fed up too, because I couldn't walk her and she had to put up with being let out into the garden. For many days, neither of us moved from the sofa. Things got so bad I ended up in Hospital on Christmas Day because of my back and had to go to the Dental Hospital on Boxing Day to have the offending tooth taken out. It really was a horrible Christmas and one I was happy to put behind me.

After finishing my last lesson for 2012, I came home to the usual lovely greeting from my girl. I gave her a great big cuddle and enthused that we were on holiday now and had a fantastic three weeks off together. Actually, sometimes it could be really funny when we were off for a long time. We could end up like an old married couple that gets under each other's feet and start annoying each other after spending too much time together. I'm sure at times, Holly was quite pleased when I went out so she could get rid of me for a while and get the house to herself for some peace and quiet. Either that or she was straight on the phone to her doggy friends to invite them round for a party – after all, there was a huge stash of doggy drugs in the house! However, after the year we'd both had, I was just so, so happy that she was still with me and I would treasure and enjoy every moment of my time with her.

The evening of the first day of my holiday, I opened the kitchen door to let Holly out into the garden. She loved the garden. However, that night, something went wrong and to this day, I have no idea what happened.

Holly went out fine and came in extremely lame. I was very puzzled. Had she slipped? Perhaps she'd gone over on her leg or perhaps she'd hurt herself digging up all the stone chips – one of her favourite pastimes. I couldn't believe it, not again, not as we were just looking forward to a lovely long holiday.

For the next little while she hobbled around the house. I felt all the way down her leg to see if she reacted, but it didn't seem to bother her, she just couldn't walk very well. I was fairly used to these ups and downs now but they always filled me with fear. I knew at some point, the day would come that she wouldn't bounce back. I kept a close eye on her while I decided what to do.

She hobbled from the kitchen to the living room as I pondered whether or not to call the vet out. I decided to nip upstairs to the toilet first while I decided what to do and by the time I came downstairs again, my patient had got up on the couch and had made herself comfortable. Although every one of these bad spells caused me great worry, in my heart of hearts, I thought she can't be too bad this time if she could get on the couch as quickly as that – and she'd pinched my seat too, so she obviously wanted to get up there swiftly before I came back downstairs. I decided to wait until the morning and take her to her regular vet for a check-up.

I have never, and will never forgive myself for what happened the next morning. Holly seemed to be pretty good and sprightly when I got up so I decided she was well enough to go in the car to the surgery. As I tried to guide her up her little steps on to the back seat, she slipped and landed on her bottom. I desperately tried to catch her but she ended up sitting on the driveway. It was awful. She just sat there with her back legs stretched out in front of her unable to move. I hated myself more than words can say for even attempting to get her in the car. I should have known better but she had seemed so much happier than the night before so I thought I was doing the right thing. Whatever problem had happened in the garden had now been exacerbated by trying to get her into the car.

It was a torturous few minutes while I tried to work out how I could get her back into the house. This time all the neighbours were out at work so there was no-one around to help me. I had to think of something else and fast. When I'd had to call the vet out in May he had taught me about 'assisted walking' where I could put a folded towel under her back end to help support her while she walked. Holly had lost quite a bit of muscle mass in her legs over the difficult months we'd just had, partly I think because of her health issues and partly because we hadn't been able to exercise as much. The biggest problem we had as my poor girl sat immobile on the driveway was that she didn't have enough power in her legs to push herself back up to standing position.

I didn't want to leave her to go into the house to get a towel, so working as a team again, I stood behind her and I put both of my arms under her abdomen and managed to lift her back up onto her legs. She was then able to gingerly walk back into the house and sit down in front of the sofa, using it to prop her up.

I was so relieved to get her in the house, but desperately upset. She was going through enough without me stupidly making matters worse. I should have known better, I shouldn't even have attempted to get her in the car. It was a real dilemma at times, trying to get such a large dog in the car myself even with the steps.

In tears I phoned the vet, fraught that I had made matters worse and telling him there was no way I could get her down to the surgery. He said he'd come straight out and arrived shortly afterwards.

Again, I was filled with all the usual dread that welled up within me every time these disasters hit. Was this going to be it? Had we finally reached the end of the road? I knew there would never be a good time to lose Holly, but I couldn't bear the thought of it happening at Christmas. I sat down beside Holly and embraced her. I was once again filled with utter trepidation as to what the vet was going to say. I kissed Holly's cheek and stroked her gorgeous head and ears and whispered words I never thought I'd say, 'you're my best friend Holly and I love you more than anything. I can't bear the thought of my life without you but if you've had enough, baby, you can let go.' The tears streamed down my face as I almost willed the vet not to arrive.

I wanted to freeze time. I couldn't bear my girl being in pain and I only hoped I would be strong enough to do the right thing for her when the time came. There is no doubt that grief is the price we pay for love.

I clung to Holly as the vet walked through the door. Despite everything, the pain and discomfort Holly must have been in, the tip of her tail wagged a little when she saw him arrive. She was thoroughly checked over as before, to ensure nothing had been broken and she was given a dose of Metacam again. Both the vet and I knew we had now reached the stage that even if there was a risk to her liver giving her Metacam, it was a risk we had to take for the sake of her mobility. If she didn't have that, we were in real trouble.

Again, I forced the words out of my mouth, words I had never wanted to say again, 'Is it time?' I then got the reply I had been dreading as the vet told me, 'If she doesn't respond to the medication in the next forty-eight hours, I'm afraid we're losing the fight.' Not once had he given up on her, he fought and fought to keep her going and I knew he wouldn't say that if we hadn't reached such a serious stage. My heart was breaking.

Forty-eight hours would take us up to Christmas Eve. Whatever the next few days would bring, I would ensure Holly would get the greatest of care. I would guarantee that every single one of her needs was met and I would be guided by her as to what she could or couldn't manage to do.

I think I was in shock as the vets words echoed in my head, 'We're losing the fight….we're losing the fight…..'. How could I possibly make the right decision for Holly when she had proved over and over again that, with a bit of rest and time, she would always bounce back and make an incredible recovery? She was most certainly the Comeback Queen.

She fought time and time again to keep going. She wanted to live, despite all her ailments, she wanted to stay. What if I made the decision to let her go, when three months down the line, she would have been bounding around again? It was a torturous decision. I sometimes felt if she had cancer or one of her major organs had stopped functioning, the decision would almost be a little easier. Despite huge improvements, Holly's ALT readings for her liver were still completely off the scale and far too high, yet there were no outward signs whatsoever of liver disease and to look at her with her gleaming glossy coat, you'd think she was in rude health. I couldn't bear to lose her to arthritis; after all, you wouldn't put a person down because their arthritis was flaring up.

I had to try and be rational. Despite the terrible emotional pain, I had to stay strong for Holly, she needed me to do the right thing at the right time, when that time came.

Over the next couple of days, I searched the internet to help me find a website that could give me good guidance and advice on how to know when to make the right decision. How would I know? What were the right criteria for deciding to end your beloved dog's life? How would I know when she had lost all quality of life?

I found a website that addressed the main things to

consider and helped me to collect my jumbled thoughts. Was she in pain? Was her pain being managed? Yes but yes again. Was she showing signs of improvement? Not yet, but we all knew her track record on that front. Was she eating? Could she toilet? If she couldn't walk very well, could she sit or lie comfortably? Was her tail wagging? Yes, yes, yes and well kind of, yes again. Was her illness terminal? – no, and does she still love cuddles? – most definitely, yes! It didn't take away the sadness of watching Holly struggle, but it provided me with a bit of comfort, there were more positives than negatives when running through the list of questions. The vet told me to keep her on the Metacam every day. The next forty-eight hours would be crucial.

Christmas Eve arrived and when I woke in the morning, I immediately had a sinking feeling. If there was no real sign of improvement today in Holly, I didn't think I could avoid the inevitable much longer.

For all our time together, Holly and I had a morning routine that suited us both well. I'd wake, go downstairs, give Holly a great big cuddle, make my first cup of coffee to have in bed while I dealt with some emails that had come in overnight. If I was really lucky, Holly would let me have two cups of coffee, but she would then promptly decide when it was time for me to get up and start paying her attention. When she'd made her mind up that I'd spent quite enough time in bed, she would start getting vocal, her cheeky whinging first and if I didn't move quickly enough to go and see her, she would give a bark.

She always called the shots in our household – everything was always on her terms. Having said that, I was just so happy that over the years, as we'd developed 'morning cuddles' into our dawn routine, always initially to stimulate her and get her circulation going, she had grown to love it so much that she couldn't contain her excitement in the morning waiting for it.

During the bad times, I missed this the most. Instead of getting up to an excited, energetic dog standing in the middle of my living room, with a big smile on her face, tail wagging madly, the sight that would greet me would be a poor sorry soul lying on the couch, struggling to move. I, as much as Holly, would feel bereft at the disruption in our lovely morning routine, which did us both the world of good.

I had to steel myself to go down the stairs on Christmas Eve morning. I was aware that Holly hadn't had a particularly comfortable night I had heard her groaning a little through the night as she changed her position on the sofa. It clearly hurt her to move. I got a little tail wag that morning, but she was clearly very uncomfortable.

I'm not sure if she'd got herself into an awkward position or not, but she just didn't look right. The worst of thoughts were coming into my head. Should I call the vet? If the time had come to say goodbye, I would prefer that it was at home in surroundings Holly knew and felt safe in. It was an excruciating few moments and surreal too. The Christmas tree lights were twinkling, the house looked so cheery and festive and Christmas Carols were playing on the TV. What was normally my favourite time of year had become my worst nightmare.

The hardest thing through all of this was the knowledge that we'd been in this situation before and Holly had *always* bounced back. She always fought so hard and if I didn't fight for her, who would? How could I give up on her when she never gave up on herself and always fought back even when the odds were alarmingly stacked against her? Given everything she had fought through, especially her serious liver condition, the thought of losing her to joint problems seemed almost like a slap in the face. I knew if I made that call to the vet what the outcome would be. I had to give her another chance.

When people suffered from arthritis and joint pain, they would always be worse after periods of inactivity and first thing in the morning following a night's sleep. They would always be better once they got up and got moving. So that's exactly what I decided to do. Before making any calls to the vet, I wanted to get her up and moving and get some of her painkillers on board. I knew from my rotten experience with my back the previous year how agonising it could be to get moving first thing in the morning but once I was up and mobile, things eased.

That was it. My mind was made up. I was not going to lose Holly on Christmas Eve. I started to rub her back and tummy as she lay on the couch to get her circulation going, then in an encouraging upbeat tone of voice, I gently and carefully moved her very slowly into a sitting position and from there, she was able to swivel round and slide off the sofa, putting her front paws on the floor first, steadying herself then pushing the rest of her body off with her back legs. I guided her down and helped her gain her balance once all four paws had reached terra firma. Slowly but surely she trod the familiar path into the kitchen and sat patiently in her favourite corner – half way between the cooker and the fridge. I'm sure that in her mind that doubled her chance of getting a snack.

First priority was painkillers which were administered swiftly, followed by her liver and thyroid meds and her ear and eye drops. We had it down to a fine art. Then, as a special treat I made her some scrambled egg with toast. I held her bowl up to her mouth to save her standing or putting any strain on her back until the painkillers kicked in. She wolfed it down – it was a great sign that she still had her appetite. Then with another carefully executed team effort, we managed to make it to the garden so that Holly could relieve herself. I walked closely beside her over the decking so that she didn't slip – despite everything, she still insisted on walking round the carpet that I'd put down to help stop her losing her grip. Holly tended to her morning business matters and together we made our way back into the house again.

From this point on, since this bad spell had started, Holly had established her own method of getting from the kitchen back to the couch. She did it in three very specific stages, resting at each stage to get energy for the next stage. Her end destination was the couch and come hell or high water, she was going to get there. On the odd occasion she'd stop en route at her water bowl for a little drink. She could be a bit wobbly as she stood having a drink, as her right back leg was very weak. So I just sat beside her while she drank so that she could lean against me until she'd finished.

So after a careful team effort and determination on both our parts, the dismal start to our Christmas Eve was beginning to look up. Holly was fed, watered, relieved and had taken her pain meds and she was back on the couch looking much more comfortable than she had when I first got up.

That year, I have never prayed so hard in my life for a Christmas Miracle and that Holly's health would continue to improve.

If her previous comebacks had been impressive, fittingly the next one would be nothing short of miraculous.

Holly in her favourite spot in the kitchen – half way between the cooker and the fridge to double her chance of a treat!

CHAPTER TWENTY THREE
Looking Forward

Over the next few weeks, Holly's recovery was incredible and surpassed my wildest dreams. Her resilience and determination to keep going was almost beyond belief. She was more like a cat with nine lives than a dog with one. I was in awe of her.

Again, it took time, patience and lots of love but she made it through that Christmas to rebound looking and behaving younger, healthier and happier than I'd seen her for years. She had gone from barely being able to stand let alone walk, to being able to do longer walks than she'd managed for months if not years. It really was quite remarkable.

She was undoubtedly an anomaly, a paradox. She never behaved in the way her veterinary records dictated she should and her reaction to different treatments was almost the opposite of what we thought it would be. Perhaps she was from a different planet? She was confounding everyone's expectations.

This recovery was even harder to believe than the last ones. This time things had looked extremely bleak. Her back legs had looked like they would crumble or snap the minute she stood up and when she did stand, she had to be supported. How she came back from that I do not know. I had accepted the fact that she would have to stay on the Metacam now despite further risk to her liver, but she was regaining such a wonderful quality of life again that I resigned myself to the fact that I would far prefer she have quality rather than quantity.

Christmas came and went and Holly had great fun opening her presents as she rested on the couch so she didn't over exert herself. As usual, she was very spoilt and got lots of new treats and toys.

Holly opening her Christmas gifts on the comfort of her sofa

The time came to pack all the decorations away for another year. Holly had received so many treats and chews, I had an idea. I was so blown away by her recovery and her strength of spirit, that I put one of her chews in the box of decorations and I turned to her and said, 'Holly, you've to promise to still be with me next Christmas, and you can have this chew as a treat the next time we unpack the decorations. Is that a deal?' We sealed the deal with a big hug and a waggy tail and put the box away in the cupboard until next Christmas.

Within a matter of weeks, Holly had fully recovered. She'd come back to me like a completely different dog. She resembled the Holly that had gradually emerged from the ten stone dog that first came to live with me. The dog that seemed for the first time in her life, to be experiencing, joy, fun and the simple pleasures of walks and cuddles. She began managing walks almost as long as she'd done when she was at her fittest. This often caused me great concern as I was so worried that she would overdo it, but there was no way Holly was going to settle for short walks and she would become quite disgruntled and start sulking when she realised we were heading for home when she wanted to go further.

She was back to guilt tripping the neighbours by staring in their windows willing them to come out and give her a biscuit.

*Holly using 'the Force' to get the neighbours
to come out and give her a biscuit*

Also, more often than not on a Saturday morning, the remnants of someone's Friday night takeaway would appear on the same grassy area on her route. If she spotted it before me and I wasn't quite quick enough to stop her, she'd be bounding off like a rabbit on the end of her lead, to tuck into the pizza or prawn crackers that had been left out for her. Sometimes it was simply bread left out for the birds, but even they didn't get a look in if Holly got there first.

She was back to being a whirlwind of energy around the house and garden. She wasted no time letting the other neighbourhood dogs know she was back and firing on all cylinders and she lapped up our morning cuddles routine again with enthusiasm that I thought would see her burst. I was so happy that, once again, she was so happy.

The vet wanted to keep an eye on how her liver was performing given the risk of the new pain medication and although I had sent him regular phone and email updates on his patient's progress, I think he too was blown away by the greeting Holly met him with when we arrived at the surgery at the beginning of April. It was the first time he'd seen her since that fateful day before Christmas when he'd come to the house, when even he'd had to admit that perhaps we may be losing the fight. Holly greeted him instantly with her wagging tail and headed straight through his legs tying them both up in knots with her extending lead. As had always been the case, Holly had her own ideas about her prognosis and was clearly going to prove everyone wrong, yet again.

Amazingly, despite the risks, the results from Holly's first set of liver blood tests while on Metacam showed an impressive drop in her ALT's – another unexpected and welcome turn around. It was agreed that with regard to Holly's current treatment plan we would maintain the status quo.

Once again she was thriving and very happy and more stable than she'd been in years. Given the desperation I'd felt on Christmas Eve when I thought I was going to have to make the dreaded decision, I marvelled at the place we had reached now with sheer disbelief. Holly and I were having a wonderful time again and really enjoying life together once more. In fact, I was tempted to ask the vet if he could prescribe me some Metacam!

Holly was doing so well again, I began to look to the future. I thought it would be really lovely if we could have another little holiday together. She loved the beach; next to the sofa, I think it was one of her favourite places. As a child, my family had enjoyed many wonderful holidays in Lower Largo, an ancient fishing village sometimes known as Seatown of Largo based on Largo Bay on the north side of the Firth of Forth. Lower Largo was the birthplace of Alexander Selkirk who had been the inspiration for Daniel Defoe's book *Robinson Crusoe*. Selkirk was a Scottish sailor who spent four years as a castaway after being marooned on an uninhabited island in the South Pacific Ocean. There was a lovely hotel in Lower Largo called the Crusoe Hotel situated right at the water's edge, nestled by the harbour and pier.

In the sea view rooms, the water comes right up to the wall and at high tide, it's quite spectacular as you almost feel like you're on a boat. I emailed them to ask if they took dogs and if they had a lift so that Holly wouldn't have to climb too many stairs - I still didn't want to take any chances, sadly our experiences of 2012 had shown me how quickly things could change.

Trying to stay focused on the positives and, as she sat beside me on the couch looking at the website for the hotel, I told her how much she would love the beach there.

For a while, I'd also wanted to explore the north east of Scotland. I loved Aberdeenshire and the Moray Firth – there was wonderful wildlife in the region and it was a great place for dolphin watching. So, again, I searched the internet for suitable accommodation on one level for us, not such an easy task as the rental property in that area was mostly old fishing cottages, small, compact and on two levels. I thought we could bear both these places in mind and think about booking something for the summer.

I had also become aware that there was a large bear conference taking place in America in October. The Advancing Bear Care Conference takes place every two years and is organised by the Bear Care Group. The conference sees bear experts from all around the world gathering in one place to discuss the care, rehabilitation and conservation of bears. The bear charity that I had set up a few years earlier had been going from strength to strength and, in just under two years, we were already helping with funding for over twenty-five different bear projects around the world. I knew just what an incredible opportunity attending the conference would be for me, the opportunity it would present to raise the profile of the Bear Foundation and the networking that could be done would be invaluable.

I briefly entertained the thought of going but it was a much, much harder decision. Never in five years had

Holly and I had any time apart. If we'd travelled, we'd travelled together in the UK. Where I went, she went and vice versa. If I did go, I'd be away for a week and that just felt like a completely unacceptable length of time to be away from her. If I went, I would have to get her Doggy Nanny to come and live in for the week, which at £30 a night would put the cost up considerably. And of course, more than anything, I'd miss her so much and if anything happened to her and I couldn't get home, I'd never forgive myself. One of my friends came up with the brilliant idea of Skyping Holly and setting up a webcam. Why not? That way I could see her and be reassured she was okay and it would help put my mind at rest.

Holly was more stable than she'd ever been, I hoped desperately that she would be with me for a good few years yet and sooner or later, I would probably have to tear myself away from her! However, it was too big a decision to make at the moment, so I put it to the back of my mind to revisit at a later date.

Winter seemed to be dragging on. We were almost into May and it was still really cold. There had been little sign of spring never mind summer. On one hand, I was desperate for the weather to warm up, and on the other, it worried me as Holly's joint pain flare ups usually seemed to coincide with temperature changes. However, despite the long cold spell, she continued to do brilliantly.

Rarely had I known any person never mind an animal with such a fighting spirit. My little Diva Holly was well and truly back and ruling the roost again. She would take up her favourite spot on the couch beside me, sitting upright so she could look out the window and keep an eye on what was going on outside her house just in case it didn't meet with her approval, but at the same time, paw my arm roughly if I dared stop rubbing her tummy for a single second. This could be a tad problematic if I was working and trying to type but I should have remembered my place. I was her servant and my sole purpose was to tend to her every whim. If I didn't react accordingly, she would get up and go and sit in front of me peaking over my laptop screen, to get my attention. No-one could ever doubt her tenacity.

Holly dropping a hint!

I should have known better by now, she expected my undivided attention at all times and nothing else would do. Secretly, I loved it, I loved that she had her indomitable, demanding spirit back and it was impossible to give her a row if she overstepped the mark. It was her single minded determination that gave her her strength and kept her going.

I was so happy at how 'back to normal' we were. This last year had been incredibly hard and the emotional battering that had come with nearly losing her three times had taken its toll.

One evening, I sat beside Holly and made her a promise. I promised her that the next time she had a bad spell, I would give her at least three months to recover before making any of the horrible decisions I knew may come. She had proven so many times, even at her lowest ebb, that just give her a bit of time and rest and she'd be better soon. Much as Holly was doing brilliantly, it did niggle away at me that we were probably on borrowed time. I couldn't ever be certain of Holly's age but she was beginning to look quite grey, not surprising given the year she'd had. When she took ill in May, 2012, all I could think about was getting her to June 30th, the day I always classed as her 'birthday' as it was the day she came to live with me.

I desperately wanted her to, at the very least, have four years with me as that would mean, given her estimated age, she would have had more than half her life with me and I hoped that would mean that more of her life was happy than sad. I hoped it meant she would have had known more love and comfort than sadness and neglect. I thought I would lose her in May, 2012, then again in September and, worst of all, Christmas 2012 and here we were nearly a year later and she was going stronger than ever.

Although my job teaching learner drivers was relatively flexible, which suited my current responsibilities, the income still wasn't secure and ideally, I would have preferred a home based job with a guaranteed income, so over the next few years, as Holly grew into an elderly lady, I could be around for her pretty much all the time and I would know exactly where I was financially to deal with any additional veterinary bills that may come.

So I started job hunting and the perfect job in the voluntary sector for a Community Fundraising Manager in Scotland for a well-known national charity came up. I sent my application in and was over the moon when I got down to the last five and was selected for an interview the second last week in May. I threw myself into my interview preparation and was pleased and fairly confident that everything would go well. I had to give a ten-minute presentation which I read out to Holly many times, to get as much practice as possible in the run up to the big day. She lay patiently on the couch listening to me. She threw the odd yawn in here and there which didn't do much for my confidence levels, but on the whole, she was a good audience.

After the interview on the Thursday, they said they

would get back to candidates within the next few days to let them know if they had been successful or not. Despite trying very hard not to, I'd let myself imagine how much my life could change, should I be lucky enough to get the job. I would have a secure income for the first time in nearly ten years, I would be back working in the voluntary sector where I wanted to be and the experience I could gain for my own charity would be immeasurable. It was a one-year position initially; dependent on funding for additional years, but it would provide such an incredible opportunity for me. But best of all, I would be home with my girl and I could give her the best care she could need in her advancing years. I had arranged to meet a couple of friends the week after the interview for lunch and jokingly I said, 'let's hope it's a wonderful celebratory lunch and we can mark the start of my brand new career.' Having had all the worries of the last twelve months to cope with, for the first time in over a year, the future looked secure and promising. I was filled with excitement and anticipation for what the coming months may be about to bring.

How stupid of me. The next day, Holly started to limp.

CHAPTER TWENTY FOUR
Crossroads

My stress levels began to rise as I waited to hear about the job. At the interview, they'd told me they hoped to make the decision by the Friday, the next day and by the Saturday, I'd heard nothing. Monday was a Public Holiday so I felt it would be at least Tuesday at the earliest before I heard anything.

It was such a strange couple of days. On the Friday there were two plane scares in the UK. A British Airways plane had to return to Heathrow Airport to make an emergency landing after one of its engines caught fire and, on the same day, a Pakistani Airlines plane had to be diverted from Manchester to Stansted, shadowed into the airport by an RAF Typhoon fighter jet, after two passengers threatened to blow it up.

In a climate where everyone seemed to permanently be on edge, it just felt like it indirectly added to my feelings of anxiety in a strange way. I know not directly relevant, but I was aware that members of the interview panel had to fly back from Scotland to London and my first thoughts were that everything would be delayed and it may be even longer before I heard if I'd been successful in my interview. It's so strange how the mind works at times like these – two potential major airline catastrophes and I was worried about a job!

It was one of those miserable weekends when you are stuck at home waiting for and willing the phone to ring. Your life is at a crossroads, you know you're either going to start a fantastically exciting new phase of your life, or you will be stuck in your old mundane routine and one phone call will determine which path you will take. It felt like a slow, agonising form of torture.

I was really worried about Holly too. Something wasn't right. On the Saturday morning, she'd been quite subdued and very slow and a little lame on her walk and, for the first time in ages, we only went to the very small grassy area near the house. Once home, she got comfortable on the couch and I decided just to let her have a rest day.

At last, the weather had started to warm up a little, which could always bring problems and it was almost exactly the same time of year, the year before, that she had had the first of these bad spells. Again, this had come on so suddenly, with no warning, after an incredible five months of wonderful health and happiness for Holly.

There was so much else going on that weekend, to be honest, I think I was in denial. The thought of my best friend slipping downhill again was just too much to contemplate.

On the Sunday morning, we headed out again for a very little walk to the close by area of grass so Holly could relieve herself but this time, she only got as far as the end of the driveway and just stopped and sat down. I knew it was a bad sign. She'd spent most of the previous day resting, so I thought perhaps she was very stiff and might just have needed a little walk to loosen everything up, but I didn't want to take any risks. It was clear that another 'bad spell' was upon us and by this time, we both knew what to do. Rest, painkillers and lots of TLC. We were good at weathering the storm together now, so we admitted defeat and just made our way back up the driveway and back into the house. I would let Holly do the needful in the back garden, then get her comfortable and settled and we would work our way through the next few weeks as we always had, waiting for the storm to pass.

I had to go to work. I hated leaving her. It was the big downside of being self-employed – there was no-one but me to bring the money in, and if I didn't work I didn't get paid and that would bring a whole load more problems. In the early days, I used to joke with Holly and tell her I was going to send her out to work as she'd have to help us earn a living if she wanted to be kept in the style she had become accustomed to. When that didn't work, I would leave the house with a parting comment to her of, 'could you at least do the dishes or get the hoover out?' as she looked at me patiently, from her position on the couch as if to say, 'Oh, just leave will you, I've got sleeping to do!'

I only had a few hours of work that day as some of my pupils were on holiday and I would be back at lunchtime. I knew Holly's painkillers would be taking effect soon so she would just sleep the morning away, and to be honest, the main thing she needed at times like this was rest. So I locked the house up and went to get my first pupil.

When I came home, Holly was still lying on the couch on her lovely colourful blanket. She lifted her head to look at me as I came through the door and I remember thinking how beautiful she looked. She really was a gorgeous looking dog. Her coat still gleamed and the light shone off it. Despite her face looking a bit more gaunt and her muzzle a little greyer, she was a really stunning looking dog. I didn't want that image to ever fade. It was the last time I would ever see her looking happy, content and comfortable on her beloved sofa.

Sunday turned to Monday and Holly continued to deteriorate. Something was very wrong. This time it was different. She was holding her left leg very strangely and was extremely reluctant to put any weight on it. She got around by hopping on her back right leg. Never had it been this bad and she was clearly in a lot of pain.

Despite this, she wanted to lie in the garden, the place she seemed to most like to be when she wasn't well. She had three favourite spots and would rotate between them all by hopping around them to lie in the sun. I put blankets in all three spots so she would be as comfortable as possible depending on where she decided to lie.

I was so worried. This time was clearly very, very different. I couldn't help but wonder if something had broken or dislocated or a muscle or ligament had been torn. I felt she may need an x-ray but there was no way I could get her in the car. Again, I felt all the way up and down her leg and gently did the physio exercises the vet had given me – all of which Holly let me do. That put my mind at rest a little as I didn't think she would have let me anywhere near her to do that if her leg had been broken.

Over the next few hours and days I was in regular contact with the vet and followed all his instructions. We were both pretty certain that, despite this appearing to be a very bad turn, it was, again, another flare up of her arthritis. It made sense. The bad spells came at three to four month intervals so really, we were probably overdue one and they always came with the change in weather. I kept her comfortable, made sure she ate, and managed her pain as best as I could. I was so conscious of what had happened at Christmas time when I'd tried to get her in the car, the last thing I wanted to do was move her.

We decided to give her twenty-four to forty-eight hours to see if there was any improvement, then we would look at our options for getting her to the surgery for an x-ray.

That night, as I tried to get her settled and comfortable, she stood in front of the couch. With her big, sad brown eyes, she looked at the couch, then looked at me, then turned around and lay down on the floor.

I don't think I can even begin to put into words my feelings at that moment. Never in four years and 330 days had she not got on the couch, even if she was going through a bad spell she would get up there whatever it took. Every night she had snuggled up beside me and now, she lay, defeated on the floor. With all the debates that rage about whether or not pets should be allowed on the furniture, it was so sad how significant this heartbreaking moment was for me and my dog.

For the next two nights, I made a comfortable and well-padded bed for her on the floor and I slept on a camp bed beside her. I lay awake listening to her breathing. For the most part she was relatively comfortable but at times, clearly agitated and in pain. I did my best to calm and reassure her as the seriousness of the situation began to sink in. My strong, resilient, determined girl was really struggling.

I continued her treatment and care, hoping and praying, she would begin to show signs of improvement. At times, she would still look longingly at the couch and I know she was desperate to get up onto her favourite spot, but was beaten and just couldn't do it. It had never been this dismal before.

I took a video of her walking to email to the vet so he could try and assess her without me having to bring her down but on May 29th, 2013, we decided there was no alternative but to get her to the surgery for an x-ray.

CHAPTER TWENTY FIVE
May 29th, 2013

On the morning of May 29th, 2013, I woke up with a nose bleed. I could count on one hand the number of times I'd had a nose bleed in my life. It may have been as a result of the stress and worry of the last few days, but it signified the start of a dreadful day.

Holly hadn't had a great night. I had lain beside her all through the night, letting her know I was there. I wish I could have said there were signs of improvement but they were few and far between, I think any glimmers of hope that she may be on the mend were me grasping at straws.

For the last couple of days I'd had my nephew on standby to come and help me if I had to get her in the car, so I let him know I'd be calling the vet later that day to get his advice and could he remain available if I needed him.

Holly had found a spot on the floor to make her own for sleeping at night and napping through the day, so I'd made it as comfortable as possible for her with blankets and a pillow. For most of the time, she lay on her right side, to keep the weight off her left back leg. That morning I managed to carefully get her to her feet and out into the garden to toilet. She was still holding her left leg up very awkwardly, hopping on the right and clearly toiling. During her last bad spells, she'd been able to squat quite comfortably to toilet, but even this essential and basic need now caused her great pain. Once finished, she moved slowly and painfully to one of her favourite spots in the garden and lay down quietly.

I brought her medicine and painkillers out to her wrapped in her favourite chicken treats and she took them. Hopefully, she would have some pain relief soon.

I put off and put off ringing the vet. I wanted a little longer, a few more hours. Maybe she'd be better once the pain medication kicked in. Holly's favourite biscuit neighbour had visited her the day before and Holly gave a very tiny wag of her tail to greet her. There was a similar little gesture for me that morning when I got up, but little else.

The thoughts and feelings that went through my head and heart that morning are almost too hard to recall. As much as I desperately wanted to believe this was 'just' another flare up of her arthritis, I knew in my heart, on this occasion, there was something much worse going on. I wanted to stop time. I wanted to turn back the clock. I wanted to delay the inevitable.

This couldn't be happening, not now, not today.

I knelt down in the gravel beside Holly lying in the garden. I ran my hand over her head and behind her ears as I'd done so many times before, to let her know she was loved and treasured. I kissed her forehead and said, 'My sweet, precious girl, I'm going to have to phone the vet. I have to get you checked over. If this is another flare up of your joint pain, we will work through it together like we always have and you'll be fit and well again in no time. If it's anything worse…..', I could barely get the words out through my tears, 'If it's anything worse Holly, if you feel it's too much for you and you've had enough now, you can let go my darling.' I felt like my world was coming to an end.

Reluctantly and as if everything had suddenly turned to slow motion, I went back into the house, picked up the phone and dialled the all too familiar number. I gave the vet an update on how Holly had been overnight and in the morning and he said, we'll have to get her in as soon as possible – we need to get her x-rayed. I called my nephew and asked him to come out as soon as he could.

I went to prepare the car. In the past, whenever travelling in the car, Holly had always sat spread along the back seat but this time that would be out of the question. There was no way she could be lifted into the car at that angle. So I cleared out the boot, took the parcel shelf out and but the back seats down to give her plenty room. I scooped up a selection of her blankets from the house and laid them all out in the car so she would be as comfortable as possible and have familiar smells around her.

I managed to get her to hop from the back garden, through the house to the front garden but every step caused her pain. It was so hard to see her like that. As soon as she got out to the front, she lay down on the lawn and I was so pleased that she was feeling the cool, grass underneath her tummy again. Her black shiny coat looked even more impressive against the lush green grass. As she caught sight of my nephew arriving, she gave a wag of her tail and a welcome bark, but it was almost impossible for her to get up. My heart leapt at this little display of enthusiasm and for a fleeting moment, I felt, perhaps this wasn't as bad as I thought it may be. I think Holly was desperately trying to put on a brave face too.

Between us, we carefully lifted Holly into the car and headed down to the vet. On arrival, Holly's vet and one of her favourite nurses came out to the car to assess her before moving her. Again, there was a tiny wag of the tip of her tail. Despite everything that was going on, Holly was still pleased to see her vet and nurse.

They both took corners of Holly's blankets using them as a stretcher carrying Holly from the car, through reception and into the consulting room. A path Holly and I had walked so many times, Holly enthusiastically straining on the lead to see her vet. It was so hard this time, to see her being stretchered in. I wanted to shut my eyes so that my brain couldn't register what I was having to watch and I wouldn't have this memory in the future.

Holly was laid out on the consulting room floor, so

she could have an initial examination. The vet felt up and down her leg and commented on quite noticeable signs of muscle wastage and felt this was what was making it so hard for Holly to get up and stand. She had lost so much power in her back leg. As I held my breath he turned to me and said 'It's not looking good I'm afraid'.

Because of Holly's health history and the events of the previous year, I had really had to force myself to contemplate this moment and think about what I wanted to happen and how I wanted things to be done when the time came, but suddenly, everything started to happen so quickly. I felt everything was spinning out of control, she was slipping away from me and no matter how hard I tried, I couldn't hold on to her.

The vet left the room to get the sedative in preparation for Holly's x-ray. At that point, regardless of her pain, Holly tried to stand, she wanted to leave, she wanted to come home, she wanted to live. She was still fighting to stay. The vet returned and asked me to hold her while he injected the sedative into her muscle. I tried to comfort and reassure Holly, 'It's just so you can get your x-ray, girl, to see what's wrong with your leg. I'll see you again very soon.'

The vet and the nurse once again, carefully lifted Holly up on her blankets and stretchered her through to the x-ray room. Holly turned her head to look at me for reassurance as I was told to wait in reception. It was the last time I saw my precious, lovely Holly, my best friend, conscious.

HOLLY, THE MAHOGANY GIRL

The wait in reception felt like an eternity. I heard the receptionist apologising to other clients that they were running late as they'd had an emergency – words I'd heard them say before when Holly and I had been waiting for one of her many check-ups over the years. I always felt so sad for the people who they were referring to. This time we were the emergency. It all seemed surreal. This couldn't be happening to us. Not now, Holly always bounced back.

There was a lovely chocolate brown Labrador waiting in reception too, friendly, affectionate and looking for cuddles. Normally, wild horses couldn't keep me away from pouring affection over dogs but this time I froze. All I could think about was if I was going to have to say goodbye to my dog, I couldn't possibly do it, smelling of another dog. Everything felt so strange, like I was in some parallel universe. I felt completely detached from my current reality.

I sat there for what seemed like forever. When the vet opened the door and called me in, for the first time ever, he didn't look me in the eye. 'You're going to give me bad news aren't you?', I said, and he gently replied, 'Come through' and led me from reception to the x-ray room. I walked in and was briefly aware of a bright light shining to my left with an x-ray lit up and then I saw my girl. She was lying on the floor on her big pile of blankets with her favourite brown paw print blanket gently laid over her as if someone had just tucked her in to bed for a good night's sleep. She looked so calm, so serene, so pain free. She was snoring lightly from the sedative and I was struck by how at peace she looked.

Holly's nurse was standing silently in the corner and I registered that she was crying and I felt so sad for her. The vet then started to explain what they had found on the x-ray. Holly had developed an osteosarcoma in her left leg. Bone cancer. On top of everything else she'd had, all the battles we'd fought and been winning or at least holding our own against, it was bone cancer that was going to beat her in the end.

As I tried to take everything in, the vet explained that the osteosarcoma develops deep in the bone and causes greater and greater pain as it grows and destroys the bone from the inside out. Normal bone ends up being replaced by tumorous bone. This could result in a pathological fracture at any time which may already have happened to Holly and pathological fractures don't heal. He continued to explain that osteosarcomas are highly aggressive and would have spread throughout Holly's body in a matter of days. The only way an osteosarcoma can be tackled is through amputation or gruelling radiotherapy.

He looked at me and said the words I never wanted to hear, 'I'm so sorry, there's nothing more we can do for her.'

I lay down on the floor alongside Holly as I digested what the vet had just said. This was it. In my head, I replayed the last five years of our lives together. The way we had come into each other's lives when we needed each other the most, the way we'd rebuilt each other. The way

173

we'd inspired and motivated each other. The wonderful holidays we'd had together - even if she had snored through the thunderstorm that had left me terrified! The fun mum and I had had trying to teach her fetch. The time when we'd visited my sisters and Holly's new found energy caught me unaware as she leapt over the neighbour's wall, into their garden and walked straight through their open back door and made herself at home. The excitement she'd had when unwrapping her gift from my niece and nephew of her trademark pink 'Princess' collar which she'd worn ever since. And the many times my lovely friends patiently sat on the floor while Holly took up the couch. But most of all, our bond. Our totally unbending, unbreakable bond. We were two halves of a whole, each incomplete without the other. How was I ever going to be able to go on without her?

As I caressed Holly's head and rested my forehead against hers, I couldn't stop the tears. I asked the vet, 'Is there nothing else we can do for her? Nothing at all? Are you positive we have exhausted all options?'

He nodded and replied, 'The kindest thing we can do for her now, is put her to sleep.'

At around 3.30pm on Wednesday May 29th, 2013, Holly slipped away, very peacefully cradled in my arms. I told her how much I loved her and what an incredible dog she was. How I would miss her more than my next breath and how my life would never be the same without her. I promised I would see her again soon and one day, we would once again be reunited and be whole again.

I was allowed as long as I needed with her to say my last goodbyes. I continued to hold her close and kiss her head. I could hardly bear to let her go.

It brought me small comfort that she was lying on her own blankets with all her familiar smells and the end had been so peaceful for her. I pulled her brown blanket over her to keep her warm and removed her collar.

The vet stayed with me as long as I needed him and eventually, I said, 'I will have to go now, because if I don't go now, I will never leave her'.

He briefly and sensitively asked me if I wanted her cremated or buried. This was one thing I had thought through, I didn't want her in a dark hole in the ground. 'Cremated please', I replied. I don't suppose there is any right time for a vet to discuss these things with a distraught owner who has just lost their beloved pet but he then said 'You can have a choice of caskets for her ashes – Pine or Mahogany'.

It was the easiest decision I had to make that day. 'Mahogany', I said straight away, 'My girl's a Mahogany girl.'

HOLLY, THE MAHOGANY GIRL

CHAPTER TWENTY SIX
The First Week

I didn't want to go to bed that night. It would mean the end of the last day I shared with Holly and herald the beginning of my first full day without her. The house was so empty and quiet with her not in it. I looked for her in all the old familiar places where she used to love to sit and to rest. I couldn't find her. Her absence was crushing. I felt completely broken without her, as if half of me was missing.

Over the next few days, I had to tell everyone what had happened and it hurt more each time I recounted the events of that fateful day. Despite years of health problems, the end came very quickly and suddenly after a wonderful five months of health and happiness for Holly, which had seen her more stable than she'd been for years.

Although I knew, in time, it would bring me comfort that her last few months had been such good months, but it almost made the rapid downward spiral of events harder to understand and take in and I'm sure there was a part of me that was suffering from shock. It was almost as if I'd let my guard down, I'd been lulled into a false sense of security, forgetting how ill Holly really was and how many problems she was battling. She'd been such a fighter, I felt she was invincible – nothing would ever get the better of her.

I was so sad, that we wouldn't be able to do the things we'd been planning. Our beach break to Lower Largo, our wildlife watching trip to the Moray Firth, the celebration of her five years with me at the end of June and the fact that she wouldn't get the chance to be a ring bearer at the wedding. I am full of dread at the thought of opening the box of Christmas decorations this year. It will be so awful to find the chew she was going to have and she's not here to eat it. I thought the incredible transformation that had been brought on by her new medication had brought with it a miracle cure that would keep her well enough so that we could have many long and happy years together.

Over the next few days and weeks, I was overwhelmed and deeply comforted by the many flowers and cards I received from people who knew and loved Holly and understood the impact her loss would have on me. I can't begin to explain how much this helped me.

I was so warmed by how many people's lives she'd touched and how many people would miss her. Donations arrived for the Bear Foundation made in Holly's memory. One supporter, who won a bear in an online raffle we'd recently held, asked if she could call the bear Holly in her honour. Holly would have just loved being the centre of attention in this way. Many of the neighbours offered their condolences. Holly had been a little local celebrity for such a long time and so many of them had witnessed her transformation. Her comical antics trying to wind neighbours round her little paw to get some biscuits, won many hearts. It meant so much that people really understood what I was going through. So many people don't take the loss of a pet seriously. Psychiatrists have actually conducted studies showing that the feelings experienced by owners after the death of their dog are comparable to those felt after losing close human relatives or friends.

People very often belittle this type of bereavement which makes me feel the pet owner suffers the loss twice – the loss of their beloved pet then the pain of people being so disrespectful about it. Comments such as, 'Don't worry, you can get another one' and 'It was just a dog' can hurt as much as the loss itself. Holly was never 'just a dog'.

I do understand that not everyone loves animals and often many people don't understand the strength of the bond that can exist between an owner and their adored pet but everyone understands love and loss and the pain that comes with grief. Grief is grief, whoever or whatever you have lost.

In the early days there were the old familiar first waking moments that everyone experiences after a trauma when you temporarily forget, when everything feels normal and as it always was. Those moments are so fleeting before the wrecking ball hits and once more reality comes crashing back into your life. On mornings like that, it took me all my time to get up, remember to breathe, and put one foot in front of the other. The nights I did sleep, I would wake and bolt upright, convinced I'd heard Holly bark which was what she did if she needed out into the garden. One night it was so real, I was half way down the stairs to let her out before I realised what I was doing. After a broken night's sleep, I would come downstairs and the devastating reality would hit me once more. An empty room devoid of any sign of life. No wagging enthusiastic tail and over exuberant dog to greet me, desperate to start 'morning cuddles'. The pain of her loss felt so physical, so crippling, so debilitating. I tried to keep busy but I felt immobilised.

Mornings had always been packed for us, we had so much to do – cuddles, breakfast, thyroid and liver pills, joint medication, ear drops, eye drops, physio then her morning stroll and now there was nothing. No duty of care. No nurturing. No routine. A big fat nothing to do. I felt completely lost and surplus to requirements.

For nearly five years, every day revolved around Holly and her needs. Every day was planned meticulously to make sure we could fit everything in, now the days stretched endlessly in front of me, all structure gone. Time began to play tricks on me. On one hand, minutes seemed to feel like endless hours and, on the other hand, I would find I'd been staring inanely at the TV screen and it was past midnight when only a little while ago it had been 6pm.

On the first week anniversary of her death, I relived every minute of the day she was put down. I kept torturing myself thinking, 'This time last week, she was still alive', and 'This time last week, she had her final journey in the car' and 'If I'd just delayed that phone call to the vet, I would have had a few more hours with her.'. Such a difficult and destructive part of the grieving process, but a normal one.

The guilt kicked in almost immediately. I felt like I'd murdered my dog. I felt I'd broken the promise I'd made to her at Christmas time to give her at least three months to recover from her next bad spell. This had all happened in a matter of days. Making the decision to let her go was every bit as hard as deciding to switch someone's life support machine off.

I felt guilty for the days when everything had got a bit much for me. When the stress of looking after Holly and the constant worry as to whether or not I was doing the right thing for her, along with the mounting bills would start to get on top of me. Those days were hard and my responsibilities would weigh heavily and I would be grumpy and short tempered. I desperately hoped Holly would forgive me and she would know that I would have done anything for her. I would have laid down my life for her. I would have sold my house and lived in a cardboard box to save her and keep her with me. It is so true what they say – no matter how little money and how few possessions you own, having a dog makes you rich.

I was so grateful for the Blue Cross Pet Bereavement telephone help line which I needed to use on a few occasions. A friend also lent me one of the most helpful books I've ever read called *Coping with Pet Loss* by Robin Grey and I would recommend anyone who may at some point have to say goodbye to their pet to have a copy to hand. I learnt from reading this book that the term euthanasia means 'a good death', which provided a little consolation and perspective.

I had tried to keep working to stay busy in order to maintain some form of familiar routine. On the one week anniversary, my last lesson of the day coincided with Holly's last few moments the previous week. I had absolutely no idea how I would manage to get through them. I had to focus, I couldn't fall apart. So that morning, I meticulously planned the lesson from start to finish so that I could concentrate entirely on the matter in hand. I decided on the training area and after finishing the lesson before it, I desperately tried to remain focused. I headed off to get my pupil, running through the whole lesson from start to finish in my head. I was determined to remain strong and professional. I would carry on as Holly would have wanted. A few minutes later I arrived at the training area, keeping my mind fixed on the lesson ahead, then I suddenly realised, I'd forgotten to pick up my pupil!

I had been expecting it to take about two weeks before Holly's ashes were ready to collect but on the

Monday I was told they'd arrived back at the surgery. The vet, who had cared so much for Holly for so many years, told me he would bring her home to me.

I will never forget that extra gesture of kindness and will be forever grateful for it. I often think back to my last image of Holly being conscious as the vet and the nurse carried her through from the consulting room to the x-ray room as she sat on her blankets and they stretchered her through. As painful as that image was and still is, in some way it reminded me of these Asian Princesses who are carried through crowds of adoring people on jewel encrusted thrones held aloft by their servants.

That memory along with her being brought home by her wonderful vet, who had fought so hard to try and keep her healthy and happy for as long as possible, seemed really fitting. From beginning to end she was given such extra special care and treatment, right and proper for the extra special lady that she was.

HOLLY, THE MAHOGANY GIRL

CHAPTER TWENTY SEVEN
Holly's Legacy

I have always been a firm believer that everything happens for a reason – even the things that we would have preferred not to happen. Holly's and my paths crossed just when we needed each other the most. Our friendship started out with me trying to save her, but she was always much smarter than me and knew she had a bigger job on her hands. The significance of each of us to the other was unquestionable. If we lived a thousand lives together I would never be able to give her as much as she gave me.

I often feel quite sad for people who have never experienced the human-animal bond and therefore can't fully appreciate the impact when that bond is broken. It is all the greater when the human and animal have come through testing times together. Not only is the bond about companionship, but also unconditional love and comfort. Animals don't judge us and they accept us as we are. They can make us feel valued and needed. Sadly, it is more likely than not that you will outlive your pet, so inevitably with pet ownership will come great grief but I have always felt it is a grief that is far outweighed by the love and companionship you experience during your pet's lifetime.

There are many positives I know I can hang onto after losing Holly that will eventually bring me comfort once the raw stage of grief has passed. I was always desperately worried about what would happen if, for any reason, I went before her. What would have happened to her? Who would have taken her in and looked after her and all her complicated needs? I am so comforted by the fact that I was able to care for her fully from the day she came into my life until the day she left it, and I was able to make sure her life was never disrupted again nor would she ever suffer at the hands of neglectful owners again. I take solace in the fact that the end was so calm for her, she never woke from the sedative and she slipped away peacefully. I was warmed by the fact that the vet told me that even though she was sedated, she would have been able to hear me at the end, so I hope Holly was comforted by the fact that the last voice she heard was mine telling her how much I loved her, how much I would miss her and that I promised her we would be together again someday. None of these things shielded me from the full force of the grief when it hit, but I know they will provide me with comfort in time.

Anyone who loses a much loved pet will go through the universally recognised stages of grief – shock, denial, anger, guilt, depression, acceptance and recovery. They can't and won't be able to 'pull themselves together' or 'snap out of it.' Be patient with them, listen when needed and be understanding of their sadness when it overwhelms them. Treat their loss as seriously as if it were the loss of a child, a parent or a partner. It hurts every bit as much to them. Grief is grief.

The positive impact of having a pet is immense and greatly enhances life in many ways. These are not just sentimental words. The emotional, physical, psychological and spiritual therapeutic benefits a strong human-animal bond can bring are backed by scientific data, case studies and hard research.

What I was able to give Holly pales into insignificance compared to what she gave me. She gave me my life back. Had it not been for Holly, I fear for the path my life may have taken. Had it not been for Holly, I would never have established a successful driving school and I would never have set up my own Bear Foundation.

She continues to inspire me on a daily basis to make a success of the 'Fostering Compassion' educational arm of the Bear Foundation's work. Through Fostering Compassion, we work with foster children who may, as a result of their own difficult early years, have started to show worrying behaviour towards animals and be struggling to show empathy and compassion. Through this unique project, we hope that we can help steer a child, who may at one point in time have been a risk to animals, down a path that may see them eventually become a vet or an environmentalist. By showing these special vulnerable children love and care instead of neglect and abuse, we hope to play a small part in making their lives happier and healthier. The comparisons are clear to see.

Although I had suffered the loss of a dog before when I was a lot younger, Holly's death hit much harder. Perhaps it was because it was later in my life, perhaps it was because of what we'd been through together or perhaps it was because the daily grind of life was always a lot brighter and richer when Holly was around.

Whatever the reason, the sense of loss I felt from Holly's parting was like no loss I have ever felt before – animal or human. There were a number of occasions where I had to call the Blue Cross Pet Bereavement Helpline and the support and understanding I got from them was exactly what I needed during my lowest times. The mere fact that there is a Helpline is such a very worthy and much needed acknowledgement of the impact the loss of a beloved pet can have. One day, I would like to train to be a volunteer for them, so I can be there for someone in the future who is going through the same loss. Another way Holly continues to inspire me.

In time, I will get another dog. I can't imagine never having another dog in my life and there are many, many dogs languishing in shelters desperately craving a loving home. Holly will never be replaced and she will always be an incredibly special dog. I would also like to set up a little Holiday & Respite Home for dogs whose owners don't want to put them in kennels and owners whose dogs, like Holly, have special needs and require a great deal of care and attention and they need a little respite. They have respite care for people and their relatives, why not dogs and their owners? I could also take in dogs for the elderly to put their minds at rest, if they need to go into Hospital. I know first-hand how much you can worry about your canine companion if you are not at your best. I will call it Holly's Haven so she is never forgotten.

These are small steps I can and will take in memory of Holly and as inspired by her, but she and her steadfast spirit and zest for life were the greatest inspiration of all.

She always kept going even though her health problems seemed never ending. Whenever we managed to tackle one problem, another arose. It was probably better that I did all the worrying in that connection and she was oblivious to her ailments. All her concentration could go on the important things in life like walking, playing, snoozing and cuddles.

I'm sure she used to play tricks on me as her enthusiasm for life began to return. More often than not I would be busy rushing around doing one thing or another and I would often toss my keys or the TV remote control on the couch rather than putting them somewhere sensible where I could find them the next time I needed them. Then as I got distracted doing something else, Holly would stealthily and quiet as a mouse get herself up on the couch while I was in another room. I would then return to spend the next ten minutes looking for my keys or the remote getting increasingly frustrated at my stupidity. Holly would lay spread out, lounging on her sofa just watching me with her big brown butter-wouldn't-melt eyes as I frantically tossed cushions in the air and moved furniture around trying to find the lost items. Then I would just look at her and say, 'Are you being cheeky? Have you got them?', and without moving an inch from her relaxed position, she would start wagging her tail, a little at first then wildly as she realised she'd been busted, then she'd open her mouth in a big smile. I'm convinced if she could have she would have thrown her head back and started roaring with laughter at the trick she'd just played on me as I reached under her big tummy to retrieve the remote and my keys. The day I lost my mobile phone, I got my own back on her a little. I rang my mobile from my landline and I'm not sure who got the bigger surprise, me or her, when her bottom started ringing!

Holly's cheeky character emerged more and more as she lost the weight and started to enjoy her life. She captured hearts wherever she went, even when she turned into a kleptomaniac. On one occasion after a visit to her Beauty Parlour for a good wash, most likely after the fox pooh incident, on the way out the door, and quick as a flash, Holly whipped a toy from the reception area and made a run for it out the door with the toy in her mouth. She tried a similar trick when visiting the local garden centre, stealing a dog chew from a box at the till, without paying for it. Needless to say, she got away with it both times, because everyone adored her and they were just so delighted to see the improvements in her wellbeing. So even her brief spate of criminal activity won her more fans.

I started to write Holly's story, four days after she died to help me cope with the grief. It was so good to remember all the great times we'd shared together and the fun we had despite the many health issues we had to deal with.

It is now thirty two days since she died and June 30th, the day that would have marked her fifth year with me. Drawing the book to a close brings an element of great sadness and with it, the crushing reality that she has gone forever. At some point, I know I will need to move on to the next stage of my life without her. But I will never, ever forget her. She will always be with me in spirit and many of the things I will do from this point on will be as a tribute to her and, indeed, because of her.

Some of you will have known Holly well, some fleetingly, some not at all. The mornings after Holly's death that were so empty, long and painful, I ended up filling by writing her book. I hope I have done her justice and written a fitting tribute to her. Thanks to Holly, I have learnt many things. Make the most of life whatever hand you are dealt. Live in the moment. Keep going even if the odds are stacked against you. Ignore your limitations and focus on what you can do. If you come across something in your way, walk round it. Do things your way, even if others think they know better – trust your instincts. Once you set your mind to something, stay focused and you'll achieve your goal. Push yourself – you'll never know how much you can achieve until you try. If someone writes you off, prove them wrong.

When I lost Holly, I lost her in so many ways – as my friend, my 'baby', my soulmate, my protector and my travelling companion. She taught me the true meaning of resilience, determination and love. My life was truly far richer with her in it and is diminished now that she's gone. I will never forget her, what she did for me, what she taught me and the gifts she gave me. I will move forward carrying her drive and strength of spirit with me, in everything I do.

When I got Holly's ashes back from the Pet Crematorium, with them, I got a beautiful little card. On it were some of the most inspiring and uplifting words I have ever read...

"Our beloved pets truly are some of nature's finest jewels, dazzling us in so many ways. Always mysterious free spirits we are privileged to care for their earthly needs. Always remember your precious pet with love, knowing that kindred spirits will, in the fullness of time, be re-united."

I really hope so.

The End

And

The Beginning......

HOLLY, THE MAHOGANY GIRL

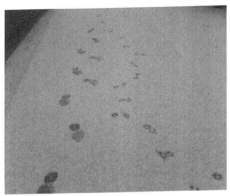

I'm not strong. She's not strong.
But together, my friend & I
make the strongest force
in the known universe.*

Until we meet again,
my soulmate,
my miracle with paws.

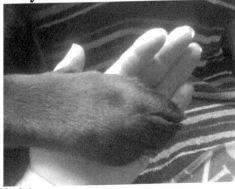

* © Linda Macfarlane

HOLLY, THE MAHOGANY GIRL

A donation will be made from the profits of the sale of 'Holly, The Mahogany Girl' to the undernoted:-

THE WINTON FOUNDATION FOR THE WELFARE OF BEARS
(Incorporating Fostering Compassion)
54 West Windygoul Gardens
Tranent
East Lothian
EH33 2LA

Website: www.wintonbearfoundation.org
Email: info@wintonbearfoundation.org

And also Holly's Hugs which has been set up during the writing of this book.

Holly's Hugs raises funds to donate to causes that help dogs in need and that help provide comfort and support to those grieving following pet loss.

To continue to follow the work of Holly's Hugs visit the website www.hollyshugs.org

Organisations that will benefit from Holly's Hugs include but are not restricted to:-

THE BLUE CROSS PET BEREAVEMENT
SUPPORT SERVICE
Shilton Road
Burford
OXON
OX18 4PF
Helpline Number: 0800 096 6606 (open 8.30am -
8.30pm everyday)

Website: www.bluecross.org.uk
Email: pbssmail@bluecross.org.uk

And

Gift boxes of toys and treats will be donated to military
dogs serving with our troops in Afghanistan and to
shelters with elderly and special needs dogs that can't be
rehomed.

SUGGESTED READING AND SOURCES OF SUPPORT

The Blue Cross Pet Bereavement Support Service (see
above)

Peaceful Harmony Pet Bereavement Counselling –
www.peacefulharmony.co.uk

Coping with Pet Loss – Robin Grey

**To contact the author of *Holly, The Mahogany Girl*
email lesleyjwinton@tiscali.co.uk**

ACKNOWLEDGEMENTS

It was a difficult decision, whether or not to disclose some of the very personal details I have included in the book. I would like to thank two of my closest friends (they'll know who they are), who kindly let me talk things through with them without fear of judgement, to help me make up my mind. My decision to open up was partly in the hope it would help others who are going through a crisis but primarily to illustrate exactly how important Holly was in my life and how instrumental she was in giving me a future.

I would also like to thank the following people who helped bring my dream of sharing Holly's remarkable story to life; Fiona Newton for her absolutely perfect cover design - thank you Fiona for being so patient with me – you always know best! Thank you to Lisbeth Rieshoj Amos for painstakingly doing the copy editing and for your wonderful feedback and encouragement. Thank you to Holly's incredible vet Ian Hemsley for his first class care of Holly and for fighting as hard for her as I did and for writing the foreword to this book. Thank you to Lucinda and Paul Hare and Eddie McGarrity for their fabulous support and guidance during the final stages of production. Thank you to Diana Street of Peaceful Harmony Pet Bereavement Counselling who believed in me enough to help promote my book having never even met me or Holly. Thank you also to Jo Rothery for her invaluable help with promotion and marketing and for always being there through very low days after losing Holly. Thank you also to the Pet Crematorium, Linda Macfarlane and Helen Exley for permission to use their respective quotes. Thank you also, of course, to all my wonderful family and friends who took Holly into their hearts and loved and spoilt her as she so deserved.

But most of all, thank you to my beloved Holly for providing so many wonderful stories to share, for being such an inspiration and for letting me be your human. You enriched my life immeasurably and you will be forever missed.

"There is a sacredness in tears. They are not a mark of weakness, but of power. They speak more eloquently than ten thousand tongues. They are the messengers of overwhelming grief, of deep contrition and of unspeakable love."
Washington Irving

4253105R00119

Printed in Great Britain
by Amazon.co.uk, Ltd.,
Marston Gate.